mental health & faith

mental health & faith

Daniel & Élida Rota

e625.com
MENTAL HEALTH AND FAITH
e625 - 2024
Dallas, Texas

All biblical citations are from New International Version (NIV) unless stated as another version.

Translated by Sophia Leys
Edited by Sarah Hauge

Designed by **JuanShimabukuroDesign @juanshima**

ISBN: 978-1-954149-68-7

Printed in the United States of America

Content

Introduction

When we were proposed to write a book about mental health and faith, the idea excited us immensely. "Mental health" and "faith" are familiar concepts to us, and in this book, we aim to expand on them, as understanding how they interact is vital in the life of a Christian dealing with mental illness, their family, and the pastors and leaders of the faith community they belong to.

To address these topics, we draw upon truths from God's Word, as well as insights from studies and scientific discoveries in the fields of psychology and psychiatry. Advances in understanding brain function and psychological sciences are incredibly useful tools in comprehending mental illnesses.

We know that God created the principles and laws that govern our entire being, and science seeks to discover and understand them. God has also revealed many things about human nature in the Scriptures. Therefore, the science of mental health and Christianity should not be seen as antagonistic. The challenge we face today is not choosing between faith and science; rather, we need both.

The times we live in are not easy. The rates of mental health disorder diagnoses have increased significantly, and the impact of mental health disorders is too significant to be ignored in our churches. Furthermore, among those who have mental health disorders are pastors, Christian leaders, and many church members and their families.

In this book, we present guidelines for preserving and improving mental health, as well as a set of skills and competencies that are useful in counseling and ministering to Christians who experience mental health disorders. We also describe the boundary between a spiritual issue and a situation that requires psychological or psychiatric help, because treating a person with a mental illness as solely a spiritual or behavioral problem would be a mistake. We debunk prejudices, challenge misconceptions, and explain truths about the experiences of Christians with mental illnesses

Mental illness in Christians will not prevent anyone from hearing the Lord's "Well done, good and faithful servant; you have been faithful over a little, I will set you over much..." because many, despite their illness, have been able to develop their spiritual gifts and have been a great blessing. In countless cases, the deficiencies, frailties, and vulnerabilities of faithful Christians in many areas of their lives have led them to equip themselves and serve the Lord better, and to be a blessing to many.

We hope that reading these pages will help to provide a better understand what mental illness entails and how to minister more effectively to the mentally ill and their families in our churches. It is our greatest desire, as children of God and as mental health professionals, to fulfill this objective and for this book to be a blessing to the beloved people of our Heavenly Father.

Chapter 1

Mental Health

Allow us to begin this book by sharing with you some astonishing facts:

The brain God gave us

During the nine months of gestation in the mother's womb, around 250 nerve cells are formed in the developing baby's brain each minute, completing close to 100 billion neurons by the end of its development (a number similar to the amount of stars in the Milky Way). In turn, a single neuron can have up to 200,000 connections with other neurons.

The brain is divided into two hemispheres, and in each of these, we can identify several lobes that fulfill different functions, from memory and reasoning capacity to the regulation of our movements and the senses that allow us to perceive the world around us.

Biologically, humans have five senses: hearing, sight, smell, taste, and touch. Sensory neurons are responsible for carrying the information they receive from our body and the external world—via the ears, eyes, nose, tongue, and skin—to a specific area of the brain. The part of the brain where the optic nerve reaches cannot perceive or distinguish the characteristic sensations of the nerves of the ear, and that part of the ear cannot perceive or distinguish characteristics of taste or smell, or distinguish those of the nerves of the skin. Within the brain, the data received by the sense organs (ears, eyes, nose, tongue, and skin) each arrive at the corresponding location to be processed, integrated, associated, and interpreted.

Isn't all of this wonderfully designed?

The mind God gave us

The mind is a completely different entity from the brain. The brain is material and the mind is something immaterial.

The mind deals with emotions, ideas, opinions, interpretations, the way a person thinks, responses to different circumstances, beliefs, values, moral judgment, memories, reasoning, and much more. Despite ongoing scientific advances, it is impossible to explain, except through faith, how the brain has the capacity to make and contain memories, thoughts, emotions, valuations, judgments, etc., and all of this in infinite combinations.

For the mind (sometimes also called the "soul"), there is no distinction made whether the sensations are received by the optic, auditory, olfactory, gustatory, or tactile nerves. This capacity goes beyond the biological functions of the brain. The mind is a completely separate entity from the brain. The brain is material and the mind is immaterial.

The physiologist (a scientist who studies the organs of living beings and their functioning) cannot give an acceptable explanation of how, once the sensations from the nerves reach the correct place (the area of the brain where the stimulus is received through the corresponding nerve), new phenomena appear, which are completely different from everything that depends on the organization of the brain or the nerves. Suddenly a thought emerges. An idea presents itself in the mind, and emotions, will, and the ability to decide are added. This phenomenon cannot be explained by the knowledge acquired about nervous matter. This capacity must reside in something that goes beyond the brain. The body itself cannot alter its natural phenomena. But the mind can do this with respect to the brain; a thought alters its entire action. Therefore, the physiologist is convinced that there is something more in the human being, distinct from the brain, to which the phenomena of the mind must be attributed.[1]

We are incomprehensible even to ourselves! And this is because we were created by a masterful hand far superior to our: God Himself. Just as the essence of God cannot be understood, neither can the functioning and scope of the human mind be fully understood.

As Christians, we use the words "mind," "heart," or "human spirit" for this, and we know that entering this territory is entering into the work of God, when He breathed the breath of life into the already formed body of Adam. We read in Genesis 2:7, *"Then the Lord God formed the man from the dust of the ground. He breathed the breath of life into the man's nostrils, and the man became a living person."* With His breath, God infused physical, mental, and spiritual life, and man became a living being. In 1 Corinthians 15:45 we read, *"The Scriptures tell us, 'The first man, Adam, became a living person.' But the last Adam—that is, Christ—is a life-giving Spirit."*

The brain organ is part of our body, which was formed by God from the dust of the earth, and is certainly something wonderful. Still, it is just material like our liver, kidneys, or bones. On the other hand, the

1. 1. Battie, W., Monro, J. y otros.

mind (or soul, or psyche, or human spirit) was given to us by God when He breathed the breath of life into man.

This sets us apart from animals, as it is what makes us bear the image of God in us! Genesis 1:26 says, *"Then God said, 'Let us make human beings in our image, to be like us. They will reign over the fish, the birds, the livestock, and all the wild animals, and the small animals that scurry along the ground.'"* This part of our being is immortal. It is what, after physical death, has as its destiny heaven or hell, according to Matthew 25:46: *"Those who have done good will go into eternal life, and those who have continued in sin will go into eternal punishment."*

The Holy Spirit God gave us

Christians have a third component, one that we did not inherit but received when we believed in Jesus Christ as our Lord and Savior. It is the Holy Spirit. In 1 Corinthians 6:19-20 it says, *"Do you not know that your bodies are temples of the Holy Spirit, who is in you, whom you have received from God? You are not your own; you were bought at a price. Therefore honor God with your bodies."* And in Romans 8:9 we read, *"You, however, are not in the realm of the flesh but are in the realm of the Spirit, if indeed the Spirit of God lives in you. And if anyone does not have the Spirit of Christ, they do not belong to Christ."* We also read in Acts 5:32, *"We are witnesses of these things, and so is the Holy Spirit, whom God has given to those who obey him."* By receiving Jesus as our Savior, and when the Holy Spirit enters our lives, we receive something that goes beyond our natural minds: It is the mind of Christ. The mind of Christ is not something we are born with, nor do we develop it with age. In 1 Corinthians 2:16 it says, *"For who has known the mind of the Lord so as to instruct him?"* But we have the mind of Christ. And in John 14:26 it says, *"But the Advocate, the Holy Spirit, whom the Father will send in my name, will teach you all things and will remind you of everything I have said to you."* In Christians, the human mind is enriched by the mind of Christ.

The origin of disease

In Genesis 3, we are told the story of the fall of humankind and its consequences. Before the fall, Adam and Eve had a perfect relationship with God, with whom they conversed and walked in the garden of Eden. Together they formed the image of God, and there was love and harmony between them. They were naked and felt no shame. We can say that there was joy, trust, and total openness; there was nothing to hide.

With the fall, sin entered the world, and with it came disorder, illness, and death.

There was love and communion with God.

Adam and Eve had dominion over the environment. They ruled over all the animals (to which Adam himself had given names) and over everything the earth produced. And in Genesis 1:28-29 it says, *"God blessed them and said to them, 'Be fruitful and increase in number; fill the earth and subdue it. Rule over the fish in the sea and the birds in the sky and over every living creature that moves on the ground.' Then God said, 'I give you every seed-bearing plant on the face of the whole earth and every tree that has fruit with seed in it. They will be yours for food.'"*

Up to that point, everything was beautiful. But unfortunately, with the fall, sin entered the world, and with it came disorder, disease, and death.

The biblical account shows us various symptoms Adam and Eve began to experience after sinning. In them we see the basis of most symptoms of mental illnesses we can observe today. These are:

- **Shame (dishonor, embarrassment, blush, confusion).** Genesis 3:7: *"As soon as they ate it, they were filled with shame and began covering themselves with fig leaves."*
- **Fear (panic, shyness, fear, terror).** Genesis 3:8: *"Then the man and his wife heard the Lord God walking in the garden. They were frightened and hid behind some trees..."* Genesis 3:10: *"The man replied, 'I was afraid because I was naked, so I hid.'"* We see a feeling of inferiority regarding their own bodies, a low self-esteem. There is a distortion in the perception of the human body given by God.
- **Blame shifting.** Genesis 3:12: *"The woman you put here with me..."* Adam shifts the blame to the woman, and she then blames the serpent: *"The serpent deceived me, and I ate"* (Genesis 3:13). There is no assumption of responsibility. It tends to blame others spontaneously.
- **Exile (lack of belonging, confinement, alienation).** Genesis 3:23: *"So the Lord God banished them from the Garden of Eden..."* We see this today in people who "can't find their place in the world," or in feelings of loss of identity or emotional instability.
- **Sadness (distress, deep sorrow, anguish).** Adam and Eve began to suffer mental pain as a consequence of their actions and it affected their happiness.
- **Physical pain.** Physical pain is another symptom that appears after the fall. Genesis 3:16: *"To the woman he said, 'I will make your pains in childbearing very severe; with painful labor you will give birth to children...'"*
- **Dissatisfaction.** Haggai 1:5-6: *"Now this is what the Lord Almighty says: 'Give careful thought to your ways. You have planted much, but harvested little. You eat, but never have enough. You drink, but never have your fill. You put on clothes,*

but are not warm. You earn wages, only to put them in a purse with holes.'"

- **Anger and bitterness.** In Genesis 4:6, God asked Cain, *"Why are you angry? Why is your face downcast?"*
- **Murder.** Genesis 4:8: *"Now Cain said to his brother Abel, 'Let's go out to the field.' While they were in the field, Cain attacked his brother Abel and killed him."*
- **Lying.** Genesis 4:9: *"Then the Lord said to Cain, 'Where is your brother Abel?' 'I don't know,' he replied. 'Am I my brother's keeper?'"*
- **Spiritual blindness.** 2 Corinthians 4:4: *"The god of this age has blinded the minds of unbelievers, so they cannot see the light of the gospel that displays the glory of Christ..."*
- **Death (physical and spiritual).** Genesis 3:19: *"By the sweat of your brow you will eat your food until you return to the ground, since from it you were taken; for dust you are and to dust you will return."* Romans 6:23: *"For the wages of sin is death..."*

As we can see, disobeying God resulted in very unpleasant consequences for Adam and Eve. By distorting the image of God they bore, they brought pain, illness, and death upon their lives. Moreover, trying to hide the consequences of sin inhibited the joy they felt at the beginning of their relationship with God, and opened the door to fear, shame, and guilt.

But it wasn't just Adam and Eve who suffered. With sin, illness came into the world: Everything was altered, nature began to produce thorns and thistles (Genesis 3:18: *"It will produce thorns and thistles for you..."*), and all of creation suffered (Romans 8:19-20: *"For the creation waits in eager expectation for the children of God to be revealed. For the creation was subjected to frustration..."*).

Body, brain, and mind were created by God, and the Bible tells us that we are made in His image and likeness. However, illness is a reality in our lives because of the fallen nature and the presence of sin in this world.

Therefore:

- The body becomes ill. Living in a fallen world, all people, Christians or not, can become physically ill.
- The brain becomes ill. Living in a fallen world, all people, Christians or not, can have illnesses of the brain.
- The mind, soul, or heart becomes ill. Living in a fallen world, all people, Christians or not, can become emotionally ill.

Every good feeling given by God was corrupted by original sin, and this can bring mental illnesses or other types of suffering.

Every good feeling given by God was corrupted by the original sin, and this can bring mental illnesses or other types of suffering to people. Love turned into lust and lechery, anger into hate and violence, guilt into despair, depression, and suicide, and peace into indolence and inactivity, to name just a few examples.

In addition, our brain, mind, and body interact constantly; therefore we must take care of all of them to enjoy integral health. Many times the mind is affected as a result of physical conditions, such as with hypothyroidism, a thyroid disease that produces symptoms such as loss of interest, inability to enjoy pleasurable activities, psychomotor retardation, apathy, memory loss, and depression.

The mind can also be affected by diseases of the brain, such as dementia, which causes loss of cognitive abilities. Inflammation of the brain due to infection can cause symptoms like sudden changes in personality and confusion.

The body, in turn, is prone to being affected by what affects the mind. This is evident when it comes to many intense emotions such as hope, fear, love, anger, joy, sadness, happiness, or despair, as they usually present with symptoms like tachycardia, sweating, hypertension, and headaches.

As an example of mental illnesses of biological origin—that is, originating in the brain—we find endogenous depression. This disease is created within the brain, without an external factor. It results from physiological changes, by chemical imbalances in the brain itself, and is not related to stressful or negative life events. The chemical substances involved in this disease are called "neurotransmitters." Neurotransmitters serve as messengers, transmitting signals from one neuron (a nerve cell) to another. Some of these neurotransmitters, such as serotonin, norepinephrine, and dopamine, play an important role in regulating mood. This depression is caused by a decrease in the available serotonin for brain cells.

It is now known that genetic factors can contribute to this type of depression, and genetic variations can be passed from parents to children. Therefore, we must take into account that a person may present endogenous depression if their neurotransmitters are altered or if close relatives have suffered from it. The risk is higher for people who have first degree relates with type of depression, although they may not necessarily develop the disorder. Medicine can restore the chemical balance of neurotransmitters and help relieve mental symptoms through medications called psychotropic drugs. At present, there are numerous very effective psychotropic drugs to treat this mental illness and others.

Another disease of biological origin is schizophrenia, a disease that results from neurodevelopmental alteration. There are biochemical alterations in which dopamine is the most altered neurotransmitter. This indicates that the disease, or at least the psychotic symptoms, are the result of excess dopamine activity. This disease also has a genetic incidence.

What is now understood by mental health and illness?

Definition of health: The World Health Organization (WHO) defines health as "a state of complete physical, mental, and social well-being, and not merely the absence of disease or infirmity."[2] This definition came into effect in 1948 and has not been modified since.

Of course, it is a very comprehensive definition, given that an economic problem or social conflict is not always a factor in generating disease.

Other definitions that we find interesting are:

"Health is not only the absence of disease, but it is something positive, a joyful attitude towards life, and a joyful acceptance of the responsibilities that life places on the individual."[3]

"The state of adaptation to the environment and the ability to function in the best conditions in this environment."[4]

On the other hand, the Lalonde Report 1, produced in Canada in 1971, says that there are four components that affect the degree of health of a community: human biology, the environment, lifestyle, and the organization of care (the resources available to the community to treat it).[5]

---

2. Organización Mundial de Salud (Global Organization of Health) - Preguntas Mas Frecuentes (frequent questions) - https://bit.ly/39YCv8F
3. Sigerist, H. 1941
4. Dubos, R. 1995
5. Lalonde, Marc: El concepto de campo de la salud: una perspectiva canadiense. En: Promoción de la Salud: Una Antología (The concept of the health field: a Canadian perspective. In: Health Promotion: An Anthology), OPS-OMS, Washington, DC, Publicación Científica N° 557, Págs. 3-5, 1996

Each culture has a different perception of what health is, and in turn, the definitions have varied in each stage of history.

Health is not just the absence of disease.

Each person responds differently to health problems. But there is something that surely all people and all cultures of all times would agree on, and that is that preserving health is extremely important. Unfortunately, this is a complex goal.

Health is a dynamic concept: A person can be healthy and then not. A person can also get sick and heal, and then get sick again.

Definition of mental health: The Diagnostic and Statistical Manual of Mental Disorders (DSM), which serves as a reference for most mental health professionals in Latin America, the U.S., and much of the world, defines mental illness as "a set of signs and symptoms characterized by a clinically significant alteration of cognitive state, emotional regulation, or behavior of an individual, given by alterations in psychological, biological, or developmental processes of mental functions."

The WHO says that "mental health is the emotional, psychological, and social well-being that enables individuals to cope with the challenges of life and of the community in which we live," and that "there is no health without mental health."[6]

A person with good mental health understands their own abilities, fully exercises their capacities, can deal with the normal stress of life and enjoy it, can work productively, and can contribute to their community.

6. World Health Organization, Mental health: Strengthening our response Fact Sheet (2016), https://bit.ly/3y3Yd35/

Mental illness

We speak of mental illness when the state of well-being is compromised, leading to an emotional, cognitive and/or behavioral disturbance, in which basic psychological processes such as emotion, motivation, cognition, awareness, behavior, perception, learning, and language are affected. This makes it difficult for the person to adapt to the social environment in which they live, and also creates a feeling of discomfort.

Among the causes of the appearance of a mental illness, multiple biological factors (genes, heredity, physical illnesses, biochemical and metabolic alterations, etc.), psychological factors (person's experiences, traumatic experiences, etc.), and social factors (culture, social and family environment, etc.) usually converge.

Mental illness is more common than believed. According to the World Health Organization[7], 12.5% of all health problems are represented by mental disorders (a higher figure than cancer and cardiovascular problems), and one in four people worldwide will experience mental health problems at some point in their lives. And, to make matters worse, between 35% and 50% of people who suffer from these problems do not receive any treatment, or do not receive the right treatment. For all these reasons, it is estimated that mental health problems will be the leading cause of disability in the world by 2030.

We currently live in an increasingly difficult world. Many people have experienced traumatic events, such as a family member's terminal illness, sexual abuse, physical and psychological abuse, job losses and income instability, political violence, or forced migration, among others. Sexual, physical, and psychological abuse usually occur together, as well as child abuse and exposure to domestic

---

7. La salud mental en cifras (Mental health in figures) - Confederación Salud Mental España - https://bit.ly/3bE80KF

violence.[8] We also see that children are highly vulnerable, leading to mental illnesses in adulthood.

Traumas of such magnitude are becoming more and more frequent and exceed people's capacity to cope with them. These traumas can result in Post-Traumatic Stress Disorder, or in mental illnesses such as depression, anxiety, social anxiety disorders, and risky behaviors. The adverse effects influence the entire personality, also producing shame, fear, guilt, and low self-esteem.

With proper treatment and spiritual resources provided by a community of faith, we can help heal psychological trauma.

Some of these people may be members of our churches. With proper treatment, combined with the support, understanding, and spiritual resources provided by a faith community, we can help heal psychological trauma.

Medicine and mental Health

In recent years, we have seen remarkable advances in the diagnosis and treatment of mental illnesses. There have been advances in the study of brain function (the use of Positron Emission Tomography has allowed us to see brain activity and its changes in the presence of diseases), advances in the study of neurotransmitters and their influence on the origin of biological diseases, and advances in the study of genes and their influence on some diseases (such as schizophrenia, bipolar disorder, ADHD, and autism have a high genetic influence).

8. Moffitt, E. y Caspi, A. Preventing the Intergenerational Continuity of Antisocial Behavior: Implications of Partner Violence, in D. P. Farrington & J.W. Coid (Eds.), Early Prevention of Adult Antisocial Behavior (Cambridge, UK, Cambridge University Press, 2003), 109-29

There has also been a great advance in the discovery of drugs that relieve or suppress symptoms of mental illnesses and reduce relapses.

In relation to the medication, it is possible to take the figures on the consumption of psychotropic drugs as an indication of the increase in mental illnesses. Looking at Argentina as an example, and recognizing what is seen there can be extrapolated to many other countries, we see f from the Argentine Drug Observatory[9] that the consumption of psychotropic medications like anxiolytics, antidepressants, and hypnotics in daily life has increased significantly in recent times. One third of women take some type of psychotropic drug, and the consumption of Alprazolam (a drug that helps control anxiety) reached 55.6% among them, making it "the most chosen." Likewise, the country sells more than a million tablets of psychotropic drugs per day, for a population of 40 million inhabitants. Among those who reported having consumed stimulants or tranquilizers at some point in their lives, the most commonly referred drugs were antidepressants.

Every time new knowledge is acquired, the communication between the neurons involved is reinforced.

Psychotherapy is also an effective tool in the treatment of mental illnesses. Kandel[10] describes that psychotherapy is effective and produces long-lasting changes in behavior, presumably through learning mechanisms that produce changes in gene expression, alter the strength of synaptic connections, and create structural changes, also modifying the anatomical pattern of interconnections between nerve cells in the

---

9. Consumo de drogas en la población general (Drug consumption in the general population). argentina.gob.ar - https://bit.ly/3a2CD71

10. Kandel E. R. A new intellectual framework for psychiatry. Am J Psychiatry, 1998; 155: 457-69

brain. Thus, the therapist who speaks and achieves improvements in the patient is necessarily producing changes in the patient's brain.

It is known that a dendrite—the branching of a neuron to transmit information—can be generated in the brain within minutes due to the stimulus of new learning. Every time new knowledge is acquired, the communication between the involved neurons is strengthened. When a person is engaged in new learning or a new experience, the brain establishes a series of neural connections. This is like establishing a new path between neurons. These pathways are created in the brain through learning and practice, very similar to how a mountain path is formed through daily use of the same route by a shepherd and his flock. These communication pathways can be modified and generated throughout life. This is called neuroplasticity.

In the Bible, we find concern for the care of our overall health.

Bible and Health

In the Bible we find concern for the care of our overall health. In 1 Thessalonians 5:23 Paul says, *"Now may the God of peace himself sanctify you completely, and may your whole spirit, soul, and body be kept blameless at the coming of our Lord Jesus Christ."*

In Jeremiah 17:14 we read, *"Heal me, O Lord, and I shall be healed; save me and I shall be saved, for you are my praise."* And in 3 John 1:2: *"Beloved, I pray that all may go well with you and that you may be in good health, as it goes well with your soul."*

The care of health in general, including mental health, is deeply rooted in the Scriptures. In fact, the prophet Isaiah described that part of the mission of the coming Messiah involved comforting the afflicted—in other words, healing their hearts or their wounded emotions. In Isaiah 61:1 we read, "*The Spirit of the Lord God is upon me, because the Lord has anointed me to bring good news to the poor; he has sent me to bind up the brokenhearted, to proclaim liberty to the captives, and the opening of the prison to those who are bound.*"

In the New Testament, we see that "*Jesus went throughout all the cities and villages, teaching in their synagogues and proclaiming the gospel of the kingdom and healing every disease and every affliction*" (Matthew 9:35). There are many other biblical texts that speak of God's interest in our well-being.

- "*Heal the sick, cleanse the lepers, raise the dead, cast out demons. Freely you have received, freely give.*" (Matthew 10:8)
- "*He heals the brokenhearted and binds up their wounds.*" (Psalm 147:3)
- "*Is anyone among you sick? Let them call the elders of the church to pray over them and anoint them with oil in the name of the Lord. And the prayer offered in faith will make the sick person well; the Lord will raise them up. If they have sinned, they will be forgiven.*" (James 5:14-15)
- "*Nevertheless, I will bring health and healing to it; I will heal my people and will let them enjoy abundant peace and security.*" (Jeremiah 33:6)
- "*The Lord sustains them on their sickbed and restores them from their bed of illness.*" (Psalm 41:3-4)
- "*When evening came, many who were demon-possessed were brought to him, and he drove out the spirits with a word and healed all the sick. This was to fulfill what was spoken through the prophet Isaiah: 'He took up our infirmities and bore our diseases.'*" (Matthew 8:16-17)
- "*Surely he took up our pain and bore our suffering, yet we considered him punished by God, stricken by him, and afflicted.*" (Isaiah 53:4)

- The Bible also speaks to us about the works of the sinful nature in contrast to the fruit of the Spirit in Galatians 5:19-23 when it says:

  "These are the acts of the sinful nature: sexual immorality, impurity, and debauchery; idolatry and witchcraft; hatred, discord, jealousy, fits of rage, selfish ambition, dissensions, factions and envy; drunkenness, orgies, and the like. I warn you, as I did before, that those who live like this will not inherit the kingdom of God. But the fruit of the Spirit is love, joy, peace, forbearance, kindness, goodness, faithfulness, gentleness, and self-control. Against such things there is no law."

The result of the fallen nature has two aspects. One is that the person will not inherit the kingdom of God. The other is that, in everyday life, these behaviors influence and contribute to illness. Behaviors that arise as the fruit of the Spirit, on the other hand, promote health.

The Church and mental health

Within the Church, there are different opinions about mental illnesses, the professionals in the field, and the Christians who suffer from them. In many cases, mental illness generates fear because it is not well understood, or because of the behaviors of some patients, which creates confusion about how to deal with them.

In our personal case, both of us were born into Christian homes and grew up attending the same church. Our parents were elders (pastors) of that congregation. When I, Elida, finished my high school studies and enrolled in a psychology course, several church members tried to dissuade me, saying that it would lead me away from the Lord and that these studies were not appropriate for a Christian.

I (Daniel) experienced the same thing when, after completing medical school, I chose to specialize in psychiatry. "Psychiatry is not for Christians, and a Christian cannot be a psychiatrist," I was told. Even later, in the practice of my profession, I read some Christian books that hold the same position. Here is an example:

> *Most Christian psychologists and psychiatrists are like a Christian carpenter who hammers a nail just like a non-Christian carpenter. This does not mean that a Christian practicing therapy is insincere in their therapy or in their relationship with the Lord Jesus Christ; it is claiming that they have not experienced abundant, victorious life, or do not know how to share it in their clinical environment. If they did, they would be compelled to repudiate much of their technique as being of questionable value and to abandon their therapy in deference to that of the Holy Spirit.*
>
> *[...] People who come to us for counsel are not assigned a classification such as schizophrenic, even though it is recognized that their symptoms could fit into that category. Such classification is truly unnecessary, given that Christ is the cure for every emotional ailment.*[11]

In contrast to this view, we, as Christian mental health professionals, believe that psychology and psychiatry can be good allies of faith, helping us better understand how God made us: as spiritual beings with a physical body and a soul (or mind). We believe that God reveals Himself in a special way through the Scriptures and in a general way through creation. Therefore, there can be congruence between the Scriptures and psychological findings. God, in creating humans, created the possibility of psychology. As Lawrence Crabb says in his book Biblical Principles of Counseling, "The truths of secular psychology are not in conflict with the Scriptures, and the Scriptures have much to say about psychology. The study of both will give us a more complete understanding of human personality."

It is an illusion and a fantasy to think that simply being Christians makes us immune to mental illness, or that all mental dysfunction

11. Solomon, C. R. Hacia la felicidad (Towards Happiness). Casa Bautista de publicaciones, 1978, págs. 26 y 37

develops as the result of hiding some sin. This argument is used by our enemy, Satan, to destroy and affect the lives of many believers and their families, who also need help.

It is necessary to understand that mental illness can be an illness like any other, and that it can affect anyone, even faithful Christians. As Collins says, "If the influences of the past and the stress of the present are too heavy, it can result in a breakdown of the person."[12]

The Lausanne Covenant is widely considered one of the most important theological documents of the evangelical movement. In that context, at the World Evangelization Forum in 2004, the Holistic Mission thematic group explicitly included mental health as part of the Church's holistic mission, stating, "Holistic mission is a mission directed towards meeting basic human needs, which include the need for God, but also the need for food, love, shelter, clothing, physical and mental health, and a sense of human dignity."

It is an illusion to think that simply being Christians makes us immune to mental illness. This argument is used by Satan to destroy many believers.

Continuing on, the group stated:

> *Lack of attention to this important issue, both by the Church and by secular society, has left thousands of mentally ill people stigmatized, judged as spiritually deficient, and sometimes, in the case of severe mental illnesses, exposed to precarious living conditions. Those suffering from mental health problems receive lower quality healthcare, diminished human rights, and higher mortality rates. It represents one of the greatest mission fields for the Church worldwide. Research in the United States shows that*

12. Collins, G. Search for Reality. Santa Ana, Vision House

> *often pastors are the first people a family calls in a mental health crisis. But pastors often hesitate to talk about mental illness from the pulpit or feel unprepared to do so.*[13]

What Can the Pastor Do?

No pastor or leader would be surprised to hear that their prayer for a sick person has beneficial effects, and that it can result in a medicine for that person's soul and spirit. But many pastors and leaders might be surprised if we told them that they themselves, their own person and presence, constitute a medicine.

Remember that 2 Corinthians 5:20 says, *"We are therefore Christ's ambassadors, as though God were making his appeal through us."* You are an ambassador of Christ to the sick person! And the presence, the word, the attitude, and a multitude of unexpected resources that operate in the encounter between the pastor and the sick person—all of these things have a therapeutic effect on the person who is suffering.

You can be a factor of blessing in that person's life, not only through the prayer you make but also through what you represent to that person! It is well known that for a large percentage of Christians who begin experiencing symptoms of mental illness, the first person they consult is their pastor. Your mere presence can have therapeutic effects that should not be forgotten.

You are a health agent! A hand that grips firmly and conveys calm and affection. A gaze that goes to the eyes and not just to the reading of a biblical text. The respectful and engaged silence of attentive listening. A person who lets the other person know that what is happening to them is important.

---

13. Padilla, C. R. Holistic Mission, Lausanne Occasional Paper No. 33: Holistic Mission, 2005, 11-23 https://bit.ly/30RnfLk

All of this makes you a health agent. But, for the same reasons, you can also be an obstacle to another person's relief. The opinion you have formed about mental illness in the life of a believer is going to be transmitted in your encounter whether you want it or not, through your attitudes and comments. It is very important to be careful with your words, as sometimes a word becomes (for better or for worse) a self-fulfilling prophecy.

Pastors, like all Christians, are vulnerable in some aspects of our lives, and recognizing this prepares us to ask for help when we need it. We should not be ashamed; acknowledging it in front of others makes us see ourselves as normal people, like all the other members of the church.

We thus avoid being seen as Superman, as someone who knows and can do everything. In this way, the expectations that the members have of the pastor are lowered, that a pastor is a person who never needs anything from anyone, who is only there in the church to give and never to receive. We must show ourselves as we are, because we are all vulnerable humans and, if we are faithful, only by the grace of God are we useful and a blessing to others.

The article "Mental Health and the Church: People are looking for mercy"[14], speaks on this issue. "Pastors need to learn to help troubled souls and remove the stigma associated with mental illness," say Rick Warren and Tony Rose in an interactive video dialogue with Russell D. Moore, president of the Religious Freedom and Ethics Commission. "The phrase 'mental health' or 'mental illness' does not equate to dementia," said Warren, pastor of Saddleback Church in Lake Forest, California, in a video broadcast on the entity's website. "Ninety-nine percent of us—and I include all of us—struggle with mental health issues, and we are not disconnected from reality. Depression

14. La salud mental y la iglesia: La gente está buscando misericordia (Mental health and the church: People are seeking mercy). Baptist Press - https://bit.ly/3⊠3D09u

is a mental health issue. Worry is a mental health issue. Compulsions are a mental health issue...Fear is a mental health issue."

Warren spoke about a brain disorder that causes him to experience dizziness and partial blindness when he has an adrenaline rush. It once caused him to faint while preaching, leading to years of struggle with fear and depression, and seeking guidance from Christian counselors. "When I start sharing issues like this, it allows my church to open up about their own mental health issues," Warren said.

Dr. Ed Stetzer, executive director of the Billy Graham Center at Wheaton College, urges pastors to openly discuss mental health issues as they would any other health problem, and to educate their congregations. Stetzer coined the phrase, "Sermons end the stigma."[15]

What can the Church do?

Promoting, protecting, and restoring mental health should be a concern for individuals, society, and the Church as a whole. Churches, as communities of faith and healing centered on Christ, can make it their mission to address mental health and trauma. They can offer resources such as biblical teaching, prayer, fellowship, hospitality, care, and counseling to those suffering from mental health issues.

Here are some ideas:

- Speak on the topic using language appropriate to the cultural setting. A pastor addressing mental health and trauma from the pulpit can have a tremendous impact on breaking stigmas with wisdom and without prejudice toward mental illnesses.

15. Stetzer, E. Sermons Stop Stigma, Plenary address via video at the Summit on the Church, Health, and Mental Health (Belhaven University, Jackson, MI, 2016

- Use the pulpit, small groups, discipleship, and activities with homogeneous groups to introduce principles that promote a healthy lifestyle and prevent or mitigate mental illnesses.
- Encourage the congregation to offer practical help and hospitality to those suffering and their families, as a church body would for any illness or crisis. Every member sensitive to pain, suffering, and illness is equipped to fulfill the words, *"Carry each other's burdens..."* (Galatians 6:2).
- Help connect people with specific needs to reliable community resources. Have information about referral resources in the area and make sure the congregation knows they are available.
- Reach out and extend the love of Christ through friendship. People with mental health problems often feel excluded and isolated, and may need additional outreach to know they are welcomed as part of the community.

Unfortunately, it is very common in some congregations for people who struggle with mental illness to receive less pastoral support, such as prayer, visitation, and assistance with their needs, than those who suffer from physical illness. In many cases, this is due to inadequate understanding of mental illness, which can be solely related to spiritual issues, or a lack of knowledge on the topic, which generates fear due to prejudice and misconceptions.

What can the family do?

The onset of mental illness in a family member disrupts the functioning of the family and impacts each of its members. The changes that occur depend on various factors, such as the family's lifecycle, the age of the patient, the strength of relationships, the family history, and the level of communication among family members. No one is prepared to face the first episode of a serious mental illness.

There may be perplexity, fear of strange behaviors and of what may come, and confusion about what to do.

In general, flexible families adapt better to the necessary changes. For example, in a prolonged illness, whatever roles or functions the person with mental illness previously performed patient performed may need to be taken on by another family member. If this doesn't occur, a crisis may arise. In acute illnesses, such as a first psychotic crisis, the impact is very large and the family must respond quickly. At the same time, if the illness persists, the family may suffer chronic stress.

There are families that tend to take care of and meet all the needs of someone who is mentally ill. Other families are in denial; they do not want to see what is happening to their family member, and each member continues with their tasks and responsibilities, denying any help and care that is offered to them. And in other families, the care falls on one person, usually a woman, such as the mother or sister of the person who is ill.

In all cases, it's important to pay attention to the siblings of the mentally ill, as it is very common for them to experience a mix of feelings: guilt for having a better or easier life, fear and anguish at the possibility of suffering the same illness or it happening to their children, sadness and pain for what the sibling will not be able to achieve in life, shame in front of their friends due to the stigma of the illness, anger and resentment for receiving less attention from their parents, love for their sick sibling, and concern for their own future due to the responsibility of having to care for that sick sibling.

Each family is unique in its structure and dynamics, and so are the responses to the problem. When a family has difficulty dealing with the mental health problems, symptoms include early exclusion of the sick member from the home; marital breakdown or crisis; psychosomatic symptoms in the spouse or children; non-compliance with medical treatments; intense feelings of anger, guilt, or despair; and silence about the illness.

Some tips for families of the mentally ill:

- No one is to blame.
- It is natural to feel anger.
- It is nothing to be ashamed of.
- Seek help and advice quickly, because it is necessary to learn how to treat the patient according to their pathology.
- Keep in mind that good intrafamily communication is what holds the family together. The more intrafamily communication, the better the response to treatment.
- There should be a space for each family member to talk about their feelings and thoughts about what is happening, and to share fears and anxieties.
- Avoid pointing out the undesirable behaviors of the patient, highlighting flaws, mistakes, inconsistent behaviors, or errors. One should not shine a light on a person's weaknesses. Pointing out a person's negative aspects is unlikely to bring about the opposite behavior, and will greatly damage the sick person's self-worth.
- Remember that words spoken in a moment of frustration or anger can make things worse.
- They must accept the fact that there is an ill person in the family, and that they have to learn to deal with this situation in the best possible way. It's a good idea to see if there are support groups or therapeutic groups for family members of patients with the same pathology in your area.
- Family education should work with families on how to manage medication, how to handle stress, how to get external support, future prospects, and early signs of relapse.

- The family should be a place where the patient can find love, understanding, support, and spiritual strength to cope with the illness. Clothing, food, money, and shelter can be provided by the family or other institutions, but what makes the Christian family unique is that it can provide faith in God's care for each person's life, love, and acceptance of the patient.

Chapter 2

Prejudice and The Truth of Mental Illness

A prejudice is a preconceived negative opinion. In this case, prejudice looks like negative connotations regarding psychiatric care or mental and emotional disorders, persisting in the belief that mental illnesses are only signs of spiritual, character, or willpower problems. Often, prejudices also extend to health professionals dealing with these issues, as the emotional life is considered unworthy of the same attention as physical health.

An idea is a prejudice when it is resistant to all evidence that refutes it. We tend to grow emotionally when any prejudice we have is transformed through access to new knowledge. If a person is able to rectify their prejudices in light of new information, then they do not have prejudices. That is why, dear reader, the goal of these reflections is to help you rethink your ideas, preconceptions, and prejudices regarding mental illness in the lives of believers.

In this field, prejudices promote discrimination against people struggling with mental health and encourage their segregation and

Prejudices promote the discrimination against people and encourage their segregation and exclusion.

exclusion, thereby deepening mental suffering. Unfortunately, in society and in many churches in Latin America, there is a belief that a true Christian does not need psychology or psychiatry to solve their emotional or mental problems, because they have the Holy Spirit and that should be enough (and in the case of not being able to solve a particular situation with spiritual weapons, it is automatically believed that "something is not right in that person's spiritual life").

These preconceived opinions about mental health within the body of Christ are primarily generated by a lack of understanding. The sad part is that our ignorance can contribute to misunderstanding, fear, rejection, or even contempt toward people who suffer from these problems.

We will now point out some of the most common prejudices so that we can analyze them together:

1. "Mental illnesses are rare."

This is not true. Mental illnesses are classified as some of the most common illnesses and are actually considered a serious public health issue worldwide. A study conducted in 2019 confirmed that a large proportion of the world's disease burden is attributable to mental disorders. The Lancet Commission on Global Health and High-Quality Health Systems, which includes professors, scientists, and political leaders from 18 countries speaking on global mental health and sustainable development, emphasized mental health as a fundamental human right and essential for the development of all countries. The commission called for increased investment in mental health services as part of universal health coverage.[1]

The numbers speak for themselves. Depression, for example, is a very common mental disorder and one of the leading causes of disability, affecting more than 264 million people worldwide. Schizophrenia is a severe mental disorder that affects around 21 million people worldwide. Additionally, there are around 50 million people worldwide suffering from dementia.[2]

Other statistical studies[3] concluded that around one billion people in the world are living with a mental disorder. Experts estimate that 25% of people will suffer from one or more mental or behavioral disorders throughout their lives. More than 300 million people worldwide live with depression, a mental health problem that has increased by 18.4% between 2005 and 2015. Some analysts assert that mental health problems will be the leading cause of disability in the world by 2030.

Additionally, we have to factor in the effects of the COVID-19 pandemic that began at the end of 2019. "We expect that the increase in mental health burden may be one of the most significant effects of COVID-19 in the long term," predicted Amy Tausch, lead author of a document from the Pan American Health Organization highlighting the devastating effect of the COVID-19 pandemic on the mental health and well-being of the populations of the Americas.[4]

---

1. Carga global de enfermedad mental en 204 países (Global burden of mental illness in 204 countries - IntraMed.net - https://bit.ly/3bwWtHW
2. 2020: Un año desafiante para la salud mental (a challenging year for mental health) - news.un.org - https://bit.ly/316hYLV
3. La salud mental en cifras (mental health in figures) - Confederación Salud Mental España - https://bit.ly/3bE80KF
4. La OPS destaca la crisis de salud mental poco reconocida a causa de la COVID-19 en las Américas (PAHO highlights the underrecognized mental health crisis due to COVID-19 in the Americas) - Organización Panamericana de la Salud - https://bit.ly/3n190ku

Worldwide, mental illnesses are very common and, the rate of mental illness will increase significantly over the years. Clearly, mental health is a current and concerning issue that deserves our attention.

2. "Depression is not a disease."

It's just that the person is heavy, graceless, boring, and lacking in willpower.

This assertion is completely false. Depression is a disease and, in fact, with the proper treatment, it can be resolved. To better understand the topic, we must understand depression as a biopsychosocial disease, which means that psychological, biological, and social factors are involved. For example, there are people with a greater biological vulnerability to depression. It is estimated that one-third of the risk of depression is attributable to genetic inheritance and disorders in the functioning of neurotransmitters, and two-thirds of the risk is attributable to environmental factors that impact the mind, altering its normal functioning. In addition, there are diseases that predispose people to depression, such as cardiovascular diseases (including myocardial infarction) and endocrinological diseases (including hypothyroidism).

If we were to ask people at random to describe depression, they would likely say that one of the most evident symptoms is "lack of will," or "not feeling like doing anything." However, we must understand that in the context of depression, "not feeling like doing anything" is not a factor of will at all. To want or not want to do something is not something the sick person can decide. To feel like doing something and then do it, will is needed. "Will" refers to the intention to act, to carry out something. But will requires an energy that the depressive person simply does not have. This energy to follow through on the will must arise from within, and not from the external context. Thus, it is most accurate to say that a depressive person lacks the necessary psycho-emotional energy to be able to "feel like doing anything."

In a certain leadership meeting in a church in the city of Buenos Aires, the absence of many of its members from worship was evaluated as "due to lack of faith and commitment." The feeling of many toward these members was one of anger and frustration. One comment was: "They must be very comfortable watching the meeting on YouTube". Unfortunately, they could not recognize that many church members were depressed or going through a period of mourning, since as a result of COVID-19 many family members and brethren of the congregation had died, in addition to several others losing their jobs.

3. "Suicide has nothing to do with mental illness."

Those who commit suicide are cowards and by committing suicide, they lose the grace of God.

Suicide is the deliberate act of taking one's own life. Every 40 seconds, someone in the world dies by suicide. But an important and sometimes unknown fact is that suicide and suicidal behaviors generally occur in people with one or more of the following factors: borderline personality disorder, depression, excessive drug or alcohol consumption, post-traumatic stress disorder, schizophrenia, and a history of sexual, physical, or emotional abuse.

Suicidal thoughts are a symptom that can appear in the course of different mental illnesses. Suicide, then, is not a sin, because suffering from a disease that can lead to death is not a reason for guilt, even for the best of Christians. We believe that God receives in heaven all those who accepted Christ as Savior regardless of their illnesses.

4. "Using mental illness as an insult is not discrimination."

Unfortunately, it is very common to use the names of mental illnesses to refer to friends and acquaintances when describing their behavior. "You're a crazy, delusional, manic," or "That person is depressed" are examples of how the names of mental illnesses are often used to describe a person in a derogatory manner.

It is even worse when people who suffer from these illnesses are insulted with these adjectives. Stigmatization, both at a social and individual level, only serves to continue the process of weakening identity and accentuating the vulnerability of the individual.

The discrimination and shame people experience is often worse than the illness itself. People with mental illness should be treated with respect.

It is also important to avoid using these terms as nicknames within a group of friends or acquaintances. It might feel harmless to greet a friend by saying, "Hey, crazy," but in doing so, the term "crazy" is trivialized. No one would think to say, "Hi, ulcer!" or "How's it going, heart attack!" In the same way, we must be careful with the terms related to mental illness and respectful toward those who suffer from them.

5. "Every mental disorder comes from consuming a lot of alcohol or drugs."

Drug or alcohol consumption is rarely the primary cause of a mental disorder. In some cases, it may even be the opposite: mental problems can lead people to consume drugs and alcohol in an attempt to calm their symptoms.

Most people affected by mental illness are careful in their consumption of these substances because they are aware of the risks associated with combining alcohol and psychiatric medication. Many people with mental illness do not consume harmful substances at all for this reason. We should not accuse those with mental illness of consuming substances irresponsibly.

6. "Children do not suffer from mental illnesses."

This is not true. Young children can show early warning signs of an emerging mental illness.

These problems can be clinically identified and may result from the interaction of biological, psychological, and social factors.

Today it is known that depression is one of the leading causes of illness and disability among children and adolescents.[5] The most common mental illnesses in children and adolescents are learning disorders, anxiety disorders, attention deficit hyperactivity disorder, autism spectrum disorder, eating disorders, depression and other mood disorders, post-traumatic stress disorder, schizophrenia, bipolar disorder, obsessive-compulsive disorder, and oppositional defiant disorder.

7. "Only people with weak character have mental illnesses. If they wanted to, they could try harder."

Mental health problems have nothing to do with laziness or weakness. If someone has problems with mental health, it does not mean they wanted to become mentally ill, or that they didn't try hard enough to avoid that illness.

When we believe someone is not doing enough to improve their health, it burdens them with the responsibility for finding their own cure, and leaves them feeling blame if they don't get better. Friends

5. 2020: Un año desafiante para la salud mental (a challenging year for mental health), news.un.org - https://bit.ly/316hYLV

and family of those with mental illness should support them, be by their side, encourage them to trust and comply with the prescribed psychiatric treatment, to remain in faith, and to continue to have an attitude of confidence in God despite the illness.

During the COVID-19 pandemic, many Christians, faced with lockdown, loss of loved ones, and economic losses, became depressed and stopped connecting to the virtual meetings organized by the church. Some unjustly commented on how "weak" they were, criticizing their behavior.

A healthier attitude would have been to ask questions and try to understand how those people were feeling—to call them, to listen to them, and to pray with them.

8. "Mentally ill people are violent and unpredictable."

This is not true. In reality, the vast majority of people with mental health problems are no more likely to be violent than others. We live in a violent society, and violent incidents are rarely linked to those with mental illness. Rather, most violent acts are committed by those in the general population, so-called "normal" people. According to police statistics, only a small percentage of violent acts, can be attributed to severe mental illness.

In reality, people with mental illness are more likely than those in the general population to be victims of violent crimes. It is important to reflect on this. The prejudiced social perception of mental disorder and violent behavior makes life much harder for those with mental illness.

9. "There is no hope for people with mental problems. They will never recover."

This is false. Many scientific articles support the possibility of complete recovery for people with mental health problems. "Recovery" refers to the process by which people can live, work, learn, and fully participate in their communities.

It is estimated that more than 80% of schizophrenic patients can avoid relapses after a year of treatment with antipsychotic medications and family intervention measures, and that 60% of people with depression can recover with the appropriate combination of antidepressant medication and psychotherapy. Today there are more treatments, services, and community support systems than before, and they are highly effective.

10. "Therapy is a waste of time. Why go to a psychologist when you can just take a pill?"

This is a fairly common prejudice, but this belief is false. The treatment for mental health problems varies from person to person and may include medication, therapy, or both.

Psychotherapy is a treatment through which the patient feels listened to, seen, accepted, not judged, and trusts the therapist's work by actively participating. Being able to talk about what is happening, rethink the difficult circumstances of life, and give them another meaning, helps patients resolve many conflicts. With good treatment, many patients who seek mental health therapy will fully recover.

Mental health is not a matter of belief. Psychology is a science that studies human behavior and mental processes related to thoughts, learning, and emotions. Psychology is one of the health sciences and, consequently, it uses the scientific method, using evidence and studying human behavior and psychological processes to reach an understanding of mental illness and recovery.

II. "Mental illness is the result of sin."

This statement is not true, since Jesus paid on the cross for the punishment that all our sins deserved. On the cross, Jesus exclaimed "It is finished" because the work of redemption was already completed. Christ paid the price of our sin, and God never charges twice. God does not punish His children by sending them diseases.

Mental illness is not a consequence of sin.

This line of thinking demonstrates belief in t a punishing God, not the merciful God the Word teaches about. When faced with their illness, a person who thinks this way might believe, "God doesn't listen to me, he forgot about me!" But neither illness nor death are punishments from God.

This prejudice already existed in the time of Jesus. As it says in John 9:2-3, *"And his disciples asked him, 'Rabbi, who sinned, this man or his parents, that he was born blind?' Jesus answered, 'It was not that this man sinned, or his parents, but that the works of God might be displayed in him.'"* Jesus made it very clear that God is not punishing anyone for their sin by making them suffer a mental illness.

Knowing that God is not the cause of illness is a great comfort for those suffering, and for their families! What he really wants is to wipe away tears and overcome death, sadness, mourning, and pain (Revelation 21:3-5).

I (Daniel) remember the case of a patient who came to my office burdened with guilt because she had a schizophrenic son. While talking about guilt during psychotherapy, she said, crying, "My son is like this because of me, because I didn't follow the commandments."

We must be clear that mental illness is not a consequence of sin. The Bible tells us that every human being sins: *"There is no one on earth who is righteous, no one who does what is right and never sins*" (Ecclesiastes 7:20). "*There is no one righteous, not even one*" (Romans 3:10). "*For all have sinned and fall short of the glory of God*" (Romans 3:23).

Sin is sin, and its solution is found in the redemptive work of Christ on the cross.

12. "A Christian cannot suffer from a mental disorder, because they have the Holy Spirit."

Everyone accepts that a Christian who has the Holy Spirit can nonetheless suffer from poor vision, a cold, arthritis, or even a serious physical illness, but when it comes to mental illness, many people see things differently.

The important thing here is to understand that mental illness, like any other illness, is part of fallen nature. It is easy to think that if the Holy Spirit lives within a person, nothing bad should happen to them, and even less should they suffer from a debilitating mental illness.

However, the Holy Spirit was not sent to us to be a vaccine against diseases, but to convict the world of sin. In John 16:8 we read, "*When he comes, he will prove the world to be in the wrong about sin and righteousness and judgment.*" He was also sent to Christians to teach and remind them of Jesus' teachings *("But the Advocate, the Holy Spirit, whom the Father will send in my name, will teach you all things and will remind you of everything I have said,*" John 14:26), and to provide them with companionship and comfort *("And I will ask the Father, and he will give you another advocate to help you and be with you forever,*" John 14:16).

What is the difference, then? Christians will continue to have illnesses, both physical and mental. The difference is that they will not face them alone, but accompanied by the Holy Spirit and comforted by Him.

13. "All mental illness is the result of satanic oppression."

Most mental illnesses are caused by alterations in brain function. As we have already mentioned, many results from a combination of genetic, biological, and environmental factors. However, in many churches, mental illness is automatically associated with purely spiritual causes, especially for illnesses that produce certain symptoms. For example, the neurological condition of epilepsy is confused with satanic oppression (we will describe this disease in the chapter on mental illnesses).

Of course, we recognize that there are afflictions caused by demons, and we know that the Lord Himself commanded the casting out of demons. In Mark 16:17 we read, *"And these signs will accompany those who believe: In my name they will drive out demons..."*

When demons act in someone's life, to weaken and destroy their life, disintegrating and alienating them from God and from others.

It is possible to detect if a person is possessed by a demon:

- By spiritual discernment.
- By knowing details of the individual's history, such as if they have been involved in occultism (the person or their family members).
- By the manifestations. These manifestations often include the person being unable to bear hearing praise to Jesus, having violent and indiscriminate bodily movements, having serpentine body movements and whistling, speaking with multiple voices, blaspheming, demonstrating extraordinary physical strength, and having an aversion to sacred things or the invocation of the name of Jesus.

We must be careful not to diagnose the presence of a demon when there is none, or to start battling against a spirit when it is only a human illness. We know many cases of mentally ill individuals who, when others attempted to "free them," ended up worsening of their condition. In situations like these, sometimes patients even end up needing psychiatric hospitalization.

When a person is sick, the appropriate response for anyone who wants to minister to them is to pray for healing. Remember that Jesus freed the demon possessed and also healed the sick.

The mentally ill are sick! There are some important conclusions to take from this. First, we see that prejudices against those suffering from mental illness are very common and should be overcome, because they have harmful consequences. In many churches, it is acceptable to have a heart, digestive, or thyroid disease, but there can be significant bias against someone suffering from a mental illness. If a pastor or leader is emotionally ill or in need of help in this area, can they openly talk about it, or do they tend to hide it? Is there fear or prejudice against psychiatry or psychology? Can a Christian express in the church that they are seeing a psychiatrist without being questioned or their faith being doubted? Can the family of a pastor family have a schizophrenic child? Can the wife suffer from phobias? Can the pastor go through depression and share it with their congregation or pastoral group without being judged? Are there churches where someone having been in prison or having committed fraud would be considered less shameful than admitting to having a psychiatric illness? Is there a lack of understanding and empathy toward Christians suffering from mental disorders? Are they labeled or treated differently than those with a physical illness?

How will believers feel when, in addition to suffering from a mental disorder, they have to endure the critical questioning of their brothers and sisters in Christ? What are the consequences if we add to the suffering caused by mental illness the additional suffering they'll feel in an environment where they are judged and not accepted as they are?

In most cases, the lack of understanding is due to ignorance, a biased view of mental illness, prejudice, or a misinterpretation of some biblical passages.

Unfortunately, we have witnessed many incorrect pieces of advice from pastors or leaders toward some of our patients who were medicated for a psychiatric illness. They responded well to the medication, with their symptoms under control, yet received these people said things to them like, "Stop taking those medications, God will heal you" and "Stop relying on medication and rely on God" and "What you need to do is pray, read the Bible, have more faith, and you will see that everything will pass." This type of advice can have terrible consequences! Would pastors and leaders say these same things to people taking antibiotics for an infection, thyroid hormones for hypothyroidism, painkillers for pain, or undergoing chemotherapy for cancer?

We must develop communities of faith that promote health in all its dimensions.

Another big problem is that in many churches, mental illness is not even talked about, as if it does not exist. But according to statistics, if a pastor has a congregation of 200 members, based on serious statistics, probably at least 20 people among them are suffering from some type of mental disorder, such as anxiety disorders, depressive disorders, psychosis, or bipolar disorders. How can we help them if we ignore or deny this reality?

Thank God there has been considerable progress in understanding how the brain works and how it becomes ill, as well as in understanding other organs of our body. There has also been significant progress in the development of drugs that can alleviate the symptoms of mental illnesses and even halt them completely. Many of these advances are recent; some medications that are very effective for psychotic symptoms were discovered shortly after the discovery of penicillin, helping hundreds of thousands of people suffering from this illness.

We must accept that mental illness can appear in anyone, regardless of whether they have Christ as their Savior. We should not judge or blame people with mental illness. Instead, we should develop faith communities that promote health in all its dimensions.

A real case: the harm of prejudice

As a psychiatrist I (Daniel) attended a 26-year-old Christian young man with schizophrenia. When I first saw him in my office, he had already had two psychiatric hospitalizations due to the decompensation, or worsening, of his condition. His father had passed away and he lived with his mother, also a Christian, and his younger brother.

I started a treatment, combined with prescribed medication. After a year, he began dating a young woman, whom we will refer to as Maria, the daughter of a pastor of a small church in Greater Buenos Aires, Argentina.

The young woman was interested in knowing why her boyfriend, whom we will call Carlos, was receiving psychiatric treatment. At the same time they set a wedding date, she requested an interview with me. Carlos agreed for me to share with his girlfriend the illness he was suffering from.

In the interview, Maria was astonished when I explained to her that her boyfriend's illness, from a medical point of view, was a long-term illness and might not have a cure. Additionally, Carlos could experience decompensations of his condition, and he needed to be on medication permanently. If he followed these guidelines, he could have a good quality of life, but he should not abandon psychiatric treatment, and he should regularly take his medication and continue under a doctor's care. Maria rejected my assertions. "Doctor, my father is a pastor and he has already prayed for him," she said. "Carlos is healed and because he has been declared healthy, he no longer needs medication or treatment."

Carlos halted his treatment, got married, and shortly after, Maria became pregnant. During the pregnancy, Carlos decompensated and had a delusional and hallucination episode. Maria and her father did not understand what was happening, and a few months before their daughter was born, Maria separated from Carlos.

Carlos's mother brought him back to the office and he resumed his medication. This allowed him to control his condition again. Today, their daughter is seven years old, Carlos and Maria are separated, and Carlos sees his daughter once a week. He continues with his psychiatric treatment, his mental illness is under control, and he has a good quality of life. He is integrated into a local Christian church and is a faithful Christian. He prays, reads his Bible, and continues to ask God to cure him of his illness.

The prejudices and denial of mental illness only worsen the suffering of those already afflicted by these conditions.

This example reveals that prejudices and denial of mental illness only exacerbate the suffering of those already experiencing these conditions.

The illness in the brain deserves to be considered and treated in the same way as illnesses of other organs of the body. It is a mistake to always associate mental illness with the spiritual realm, assuming it is a consequence of sin or a satanic attack. Brain illnesses are bodily illnesses like any other and need to be diagnosed and often treated by medicine.

Chapter 3

Faith as a resource within mental illness

In Hebrews 11:1 we read, "Faith is the assurance of things hoped for, the conviction of things not seen." And so it is: Faith involves the assurance and conviction of things we do not see.

Human reasoning and what we perceive through our senses has a significant influence on our daily lives, but it has nothing to do with faith. Our environment and difficult experiences impact our lives; we observe this reality, analyze it, and try to draw our conclusions, which we consider to be true. Faith does not work that way.

For some reason, people need to put their faith in something when illness appears. We see that countless amulets, prints, phrases, and beliefs are used for this type of support. But we read in Ezekiel 13:18 the following warning: "*Thus says the Lord God: 'Woe to the women who sew magic bands upon all wrists, and make veils for the heads of persons of every stature, in the hunt for souls! Will you hunt down souls belonging to my people, and keep your own souls alive? You have profaned me among my people for handfuls of barley and for pieces of bread, putting to death souls that should not die and keeping alive souls that should not live, by your lying to my people, who listen to lies.'"*

It is common for the loss of health, and even more the loss of mental health, to mobilize the person and their family to seek help and support in outside of themselves. However, the only thing that can truly sustain us in the midst of illness is not something we can touch or see. It is the Holy Spirit and the promises we find in the Word of God.

Having faith means delegating all truth to God. To delegate is to give God the role, the authority, and the power to declare the truth on our behalf, beyond our desire and reasoning. This is why we say that all truth is God's truth.

In John 18:37-38 we read a very interesting conversation:

> *"Pilate said to him, 'So you are a king?'*
>
> *Jesus answered, 'You say that I am a king. For this I was born and for this I came into the world, to testify to the truth. Everyone who belongs to the truth listens to my voice.'*
>
> *Pilate asked him, 'What is the truth?'..."*

As we know, in John 14:6 Jesus had already answered this question by saying, *"I am the way, and the truth, and the life. No one comes to the Father except through me."*

Therefore, we must always bear in mind, through faith, that God's truth goes beyond our senses and reason, even if they are in conflict. Faith leads us to believe in the full truth of the Word of God—and not only to believe but also to love it!

Having faith is believing that all the promises of God are true. And living in the truth of the Word of God brings total security to our lives.

In Proverbs 3:5-6 it says, *"Trust in the Lord with all your heart, and do not rely on your own insight. In all your ways acknowledge him, and he will make straight your paths."*

Paul also warns us that, as Christians, our faith can be deceived. We read in 2 Corinthians 11:3-4, *"But I am afraid that as the serpent deceived Eve by his cunning, your thoughts will be led astray from a sincere and pure devotion to Christ."* You are being led astray.

Living in the truth of God's Word brings total security to our lives.

Christians can sometimes get distracted by looking around or focusing on the difficult circumstances they are going through and drawing conclusions from what they see. This is what happened to the disciples who were with Jesus in the boat crossing the Sea of Galilee. We know how that story ends. When they reached the region of the Gadarenes, there was a man who needed Him to be there. Everything God does has a purpose. Jesus knew this well. The disciples did not know, but Jesus had a mission. The man was set free. When he wanted to follow Jesus, Jesus did not allow it, but told the man to stay in the Decapolis. There the man testified of his faith, and ten churches were built as a result of his message. That boat was heading in the right direction, in the direction of God's will, with a purpose and the right people!

However, a great storm arose in the middle of the journey. They were experienced fishermen and knew about storms, but evidently, this felt different. The disciples were afraid they would sink. They could not handle the boat. Jesus wanted to teach them a practical lesson, and tested their faith in the realm of their daily lives, in an area where they ordinarily knew what to do. But He didn't allow them to go through a situation more difficult than they could bear. (Don't forget: when storms come into our lives, He may want to teach us a practical lesson. We do not know our limits, but God knows how far He can take us with that storm, and how long He wants us to go through it).

But let's go back to the biblical account. Jesus was sleeping. It was a great lake, a small sea. The Sea of Galilee is about 8-12 kilometers long, about 21 kilometers wide, and about 48 meters deep. In desperation, fearing death, the disciples went to where Jesus was sleeping and, crying out, woke Him up asking for help: "Teacher! Don't you care that we drown? How can you keep sleeping in this situation? As we clearly see in this passage, the normal reaction of the Christian in the face of a storm or an unexpected problem is usually surprise, confusion, fear, and asking the Lord for help (and even confronting Him if He seems indifferent).

Jesus asked them, "*...why are you so afraid?*" (Matthew 8:26, NIV). Or, in other words, where is your faith? How is it that you do not have faith? Do you not believe that I can calm this storm?

Peter, who lived through this experience in the boat, learned this lesson. Years later, in one of his letters, Peter wrote, "*Cast all your anxiety on him because he cares for you*" (1 Peter 5:7, NIV). The fear the disciples felt in the face of the danger of death was natural and even instinctive. Like the disciples, we also let ourselves be carried away by natural emotions and reasoning. That is why we need to learn to live by faith. Many times when we are in the middle of the storm, we do not have the ability to think clearly. That is why it is important to prepare in advance for when the storms come, knowing the promises of His Word.

After Jesus calmed the sea, they asked themselves a question: "The disciples were amazed and asked, "*Who is this, that even the winds and the sea obey him?*" (Matthew 8:27). What image do you have of your life right now, at this moment? Are you taking water out of your boat and shouting "I'm sinking, I'm sinking!"? Or are you thinking, feeling, and declaring that if Jesus is in the boat with you, then you can have peace? He is sovereign and knows what you are going through. Leave the whys and wherefores aside, because they are questions that probably cannot be answered in the moment. The storm is not the time to answer questions; it is the time to put all your trust in Him and say, "Glory to God because He is in my boat!" As long as we are alive, there will be storms. But in those moments, we can stand in faith.

We need to listen to what God says through His Word. God has spoken and still speaks! We must stop listening only to logical thoughts and reasoning about our circumstances, and learn instead to listen by faith to the voice of God speaking to our spirit. God created all things by the power of His Word, and we are the people of the Word. That is why it is important to have good ears to listen to God. The most frequent phrase in the Old Testament is *"Thus says the Lord" or "The word of the Lord came to me saying..."* And the first lesson that Samuel learned was *"...Speak, Lord, for your servant is listening"* (1 Samuel 3:10).

Faith is the conviction of what is not seen. Eyesight is not a compass for our life. The eyes of faith are the compass, focused on all the promises we find in His Word. The Word of the Lord is to be received and believed! Therefore, Christian faith, the one that can sustain us in the midst of pain and illness, is not based on circumstances, on what we see, or on what we reason with our natural mind, but on what God has spoken through His Word. We must trust in God's revelation when our thoughts contradict the Bible! Our convictions must come from our heart, not from our natural mind. In the face of the most difficult situations we may experience, we have the Holy Spirit, who will help us to think about what happens to us from the perspective of Christ.

In 1 Corinthians 2:13 (NIV) it says: *"This is what we speak, not in words taught us by human wisdom but in words taught by the Spirit, explaining spiritual realities with Spirit-taught words."* Faith is seeing things with the mind of Christ and viewing reality from that perspective.

Returning to the theme of this book, as Christians, and based on what we read in the Word of God, we know that faith in the God who is love, faithful, and all-powerful is a source of help, support, and strength in times of illness. Faith gives strength. That is why it is a source of resistance, resilience, and restoration for those who suffer. When one has faith, mental illnesses are overcome with greater resilience.

Faith in the loving, faithful, and all-powerful God is a help, support, and strength in the face of fear.

The path of faith goes from uncertainty to certainty, from hopelessness to hope, and has a definitive goal, the point where we meet with Christ and faith will no longer be necessary. In the meantime, we need it throughout life and in all circumstances. In good times and in difficult ones, in health and in illness.

Next, we will detail the support that faith provides in difficult times of mental illness:

Faith helps to resist fears and apprehensions by holding onto the faithfulness of God and His promises.

Fear is present in many mental illnesses, not only in the people who suffer from them but also in their families. Fear can manifest in panic disorders, phobias, acute anxiety crises, auditory and visual hallucinations, and in obsessive disorders when the person cannot fulfill their rituals and fears that something bad will happen.

On numerous occasions, Jesus told His disciples, *"Do not be afraid."*

He knew that fear is a very common negative emotion, one that originated in the Garden of Eden when Adam and Eve disobeyed and then hid from God. In the Bible, we find references to "do not fear" more than 360 times. In what sense is faith a useful tool for facing this harmful emotion? It's simple. Faith helps to resist fears, and reminds us to cling to God's faithfulness and promises.

Psalm 46:1 says, *"God is our refuge and strength, an ever-present help in trouble."* In Deuteronomy 31:8 we read, *"The Lord himself goes before you and will be with you; he will never leave you nor forsake you. Do not be afraid; do not be discouraged."* Remembering that the Lord God is great and powerful helps us to overcome fear.

At one point, the psalmist asks if it is right to be afraid if we trust in God: *"In God I trust and am not afraid..."* (Psalm 56:11). Jesus asked His disciples the same question when they were very scared in the boat in the middle of the storm. He made them think by asking, *"You of little faith, why are you so afraid?"* (Matthew 8:26).

To trust is to be supported by God even when everything is shaking. *"When I am afraid, I put my trust in you"* (Psalm 56:3).

Faith in God and trust in His promises deliver us from fear in the midst of illness.

The faith in the loving, faithful, and all-powerful God is a support against the stress of the sick and their family members.

Stress is a mental and physical reaction that arises when a situation exceeds our capacity to cope with it. It involves physiological and psychological mechanisms that are triggered when control over the environment is lost, when a problem cannot be faced, or when the best way to face a problem isn't known. This occurs very frequently in families when one of their members begins to manifest a mental illness. It is a new situation for everyone, and it is difficult to understand what is happening, how it will evolve, if it will be cured, and how to treat the person who is suffering. The mental illness of a family member mobilizes and strongly impacts the life, mind, and emotions of everyone around them, generating a lot of stress. However, through faith the sick person and their family can seek refuge in God, trusting that God will never put them in a situation that they cannot resist.

Anxiety is one of the primary reactions to stress, but we must always remember the advice of the apostle Peter: "*Cast all your anxieties on him, because he cares for you*" (1 Peter 5:7, NIV).

The faith in the loving, faithful, and almighty God, mitigates feelings of sadness.

We all know how it feels to be sad. But having a constant feeling of sadness is truly overwhelming. In Proverbs 15:30 we read, "*A cheerful look brings joy to the heart, and good news gives new strength.*" There is very good news that we can give to the sick who are sunk in sadness! When you are in front of one of them, look at them with a loving face, because you will always be a bearer of hope and good news for them on behalf of a God who loves them!

Sadness and hopelessness are overcome by faith in a God who is loving and almighty. The sick will receive new strength when you tell them about the love and care God has for their life.

Sadness and hopelessness take away strength and steal energy, but faith full of hope uplifts the spirit, renews strength, gives new enthusiasm, and opens the mind to see new options and alternatives to cope with or confront an illness. As it says in Romans 12:12, "*Be joyful in hope, patient in affliction, faithful in prayer.*" Hope in the Lord brings joy and removes sadness! Psalm 94:19 says, "*When anxiety was great within me, your consolation brought me joy.*" The Lord not only comforts with relief from sorrow, but also with the joy of His presence.

Another precious verse to share with someone who is suffering is Isaiah 61:10: "*The prophet says: Let me tell you about the joy that God has given me! He has clothed me with garments of salvation and arrayed me in a robe of righteousness, as a bridegroom adorns his head like a priest, and as a bride adorns herself with her jewels.*" When you remind a sick person that God, in saving and justifying them with the precious blood of Christ, has dressed them for a feast, their face will probably hint at a smile!

Faith in the loving, faithful, and all-powerful God helps to avoid discouragement and despair.

Discouragement is the lack of desire or energy to continue doing something. Sustaining a mental illness for an extended period of time can discourage many people, and even lead them to lack the will to keep living. But Psalm 34:17-19 says, "*The righteous cry out, and the Lord hears them; he delivers them from all their troubles. The Lord is close to the brokenhearted and saves those who are crushed in spirit. The righteous person may have many troubles, but the Lord delivers him from them all.*"

In Proverbs 18:14 we read, "*The human spirit can endure in sickness, but a crushed spirit who can bear?*" Discouragement, despondency, hopelessness, exhaustion, and prostration are very difficult to sustain and manage. If we encounter a mentally ill person who is also downcast, the main tool we have at our disposal to help them is faith in God. Psalm 42:11 says, "*Why, my soul, are you downcast? Why so disturbed within me? Put your hope in God, for I will yet praise him, my Savior and my God.*"

The person who has faith overcomes despondency and discouragement because through faith they have hope in God, in His love and

His power. The broken emotions are bandaged by the divine and beloved physician. As Psalm 147:3 says, "*He heals the brokenhearted and binds up their wounds.*" If the sick person or their family feel emotionally broken, or if they feel that a situation is too heavy, in His presence they can find rest, encouragement, and strength.

Faith in the loving, faithful, and all-powerful God is a help, support, and strength in the face of feelings of loneliness.

The mentally ill tend to isolate themselves. Many of them do not leave their homes, and others do not leave their bedroom because they have no desire to communicate with anyone. They feel misunderstood by those around them and seek the security of their room to avoid a hostile environment. Many of them lack the ability to face interpersonal relationships, which makes them feel lonely. For these cases, there are also precious promises in the Word of God:

> "*Do not be afraid because the Lord will go ahead of you and be with you. He will not forsake you. Do not be afraid or discouraged*" (Deuteronomy 31:8).
>
> "*I will be with you [...] I will not fail you or abandon you, nor will I leave you without help*" (Joshua 1:5).
>
> "*Do not be afraid, for I am with you, do not be discouraged. I am your God, I will strengthen you, I will help you, I will uphold you with my triumphant right hand*" (Isaiah 41:10).
>
> "*...I am with you always, even to the end of the world*" (Matthew 28:20).

These promises tell us that He is with each of His children every day, that He never fails or abandons us, that He goes ahead showing the way, and walks beside us, taking us by the hand.

Faith in the loving, faithful, and all-powerful God provides strength in emotional pain.

Emotional pain is a psychic wound that no one sees, but it causes great internal suffering. It is common for the mentally ill to feel weak and vulnerable due to their limitations, but by putting their faith in Christ, they are strengthened and bring to life the words of the apostle Paul when he said: *"I can do all things through Christ who strengthens me"* (Philippians 4:13). Faith strengthens them!

Often, those suffering from mental illness experience emotional breakdowns that weaken them in every aspect. In those moments, having faith can provide them with refuge from their emotional chaos. Psalm 9:9 says, *"The Lord is a refuge for the oppressed, a stronghold in times of trouble."*

When an ill person carries their symptoms for a long time, they may feel like their strength to continue is running out. They feel weak, fragile, and full of and emotional pain. But by renewing their faith in Christ, they can recognize that the power of God acts in the midst of human pain and fragility: *"...My grace is sufficient for you, for my power is made perfect in weakness..."* (2 Corinthians 12:9).

There is a close relationship between illness and the strength of faith. James 1:3 says, *"because you know that the testing of your faith produces perseverance."* Faith sustains the sick in the midst of emotional pain, helping them to stand firm with their eyes only on God. This way, they feel that God strengthens, helps, and holds them in a way that is almost inexplicable.

The power of God works in the midst of pain, often not to take it away, but to bear it with faith in divine power.

As we read in Isaiah 41:10, *"Fear not, for I am with you; be not dismayed, for I am your God; I will strengthen you, I will help you, I will uphold you with my righteous right hand."* The power of God works in the midst of pain, often not to remove it, but to endure it with faith in divine power. The Lord renews strength and hope to continue day by day.

Faith in the loving, faithful, and all-powerful God helps the sick person to understand that their value as a person remains intact.

We understand self-esteem as the valuation a person has for themselves. Unfortunately, there is a strong relationship between mental illness and low self-esteem. There is nothing that destroys a person with a mental disorder more than believing they are of little value. We must help them understand that no person is of little value to God! Everyone has value and dignity to Him. And God, with His unconditional love, always dignifies people.

Every person, including those with mental illness, bears the seal of God's creation, and God says that everything He made is very good. Through faith, the sick person can recognize that despite their illness, God made them in His image, just as He made everyone else. When a person recognizes that their identity is in Christ, this carries much more weight than the illness they suffer from. The illness is just a trial they must endure, one that God can even transform into a blessing.

It is possible for the mentally ill to overcome rejection and contempt from others, and even self-contempt, when they are sure of the value they have for God, and of the love and acceptance of their Heavenly Father.

Faith in the loving, faithful, and all-powerful God helps the sick person to overcome distorted thoughts.

Distorted thoughts are negative, destructive, or paralyzing and can condition the life of the someone with mental illness. Examples of these kinds of thoughts include "It's my fault," "God abandoned me," "I'm a wretch," "There's no way out for me," and others.

One of the battlefronts for the mentally ill is their thoughts. Their thoughts influence their decisions and actions. But it is possible to destroy distorted thoughts through faith in God!

We can find different distorted thoughts in mental illnesses:

1. Thoughts of ruin, where everything that will come is catastrophic.
2. Thoughts of harm, where the patient feels that everything that happens to them is someone else's fault.
3. Thoughts of sadness, characteristic of depressive disorders, which lead the patient to frequent crying.
4. Mental rumination, characteristic of anxiety disorders, which occurs when the mind is focused on a fixed idea that causes discomfort, stress, and anxiety. The thought is like a wheel always turning on the same thing.
5. Obsessive thoughts, characteristic of obsessive disorders. These are very negative thoughts that appear in the mind without being sought, and they generate great anxiety thinking that they may be true. People struggle to remove them from their mind, usually without success.
6. Disorganized thoughts, characteristic of psychosis. They are false beliefs not based on reality. Pathological, erroneous thoughts lead to distorted judgment that does not discern reality. One thing is perceived and said in place of another.

A practice the mentally ill can do to help themselves is to write negative thoughts on paper and then, immediately following, write: "This thought is not true, not correct, and does not belong to me. The correct thought is..." and then write the opposite of what was written before.

Another way to displace unhealthy thoughts from the mind with healthy ones is to follow biblical advice. The Bible urges us to do this in Philippians 4:8: *"Finally, brothers and sisters, whatever is true, whatever is noble, whatever is right, whatever is pure, whatever is lovely, whatever is admirable—if anything is excellent or praiseworthy—think about such things."*

Faith helps the patient develop good thoughts that come from the Word of God. Faith in God and the guidance of the Holy Spirit will help them think according to what Christ has for their life! That is why it is so important to read the Bible frequently. If it is difficult to read, listening to an audio version of the Bible can be a good alternative.

Thoughts are generated by ideas. A chain of ideas forms a thought, a chain of thoughts forms a judgment, and judgments form reasoning. With judgments, value is given to things: if they are correct or incorrect, if they are good or bad, if they are pleasant or unpleasant. When associating judgments the mind is reasoning, and reasoning is the human being's highest cognitive capacity.

But where do ideas come from in the first place? Ideas come from interests, learning, what is heard, seen, and read... That is why it is so important to pay attention to things, because everything that is seen or heard will generate ideas in the mind, which will ultimately condition life.

Good thoughts generate good emotions and behaviors. And as Romans 8:6 says, *"The mind governed by the Spirit is life and peace..."*

Faith in the God of love, faithful and all-powerful, helps us to accept the reality of illness without seeking explanations for unanswerable questions.

A healing concept is that of acceptance. Acceptance doesn't mean approving, in the sense of qualifying the illness that causes suffering as good or positive. Acceptance means receiving and integrating suffering, or the reason that caused it, into one's own life, as an experience or as part of one's own history. In the case of the family, acceptance allows for mobilization toward helping the sick person.

Acceptance also implies recognizing the emotions that arise in the family environment without denying or avoiding feelings. Accepting a family member's illness promotes action: analyzing the available resources and channeling them to begin to navigate the paths the presence of the illness requires. Accepting the illness can prevent the mental and emotional energy from draining from a family member as they seek to care for a loved one who is suffering.

Faith helps us to accept the timing and purposes of God even in the midst of suffering from illness.

Faith helps to accept God's timing and purposes even in illness. God does not punish us with suffering or illness. God always gives guidance and strength to anyone who is suffering and to their family. God always gives grace to endure suffering in times of pain.

Acceptance also means letting go of expectations that cannot be fulfilled. For example, a family has expectations that their son will become an engineer like his father, but the son begins suffering from schizophrenia during his adolescence with a psychotic episode. The illness continues over the years, leaving him unable to attend university. The father, out of frustration, cannot accept the reality of his son's illness, demands things from him, and frequently gets angry with him, worsening his health.

When, through faith, the father accepts the situation, the questioning and "whys" directed toward the Lord cease. With faith in the loving and almighty God, one can accept what has happened even without understanding the reasons. Living by faith means not seeking explanations. In 2 Corinthians 5:7 it says, *"For we walk by faith, not by sight."* We also see in many biblical characters how faith helped them accept difficult realities without answers (for example, Job had no answer to his suffering).

The opposite of accepting illness is denying it. Denial occurs when one does not want to, or cannot, see something for what it is. For example: "Nothing's wrong here, my husband is not ill. He just has some character issues." With mental illness, there aren't physical symptoms showing that the person is ill. There is no fever, they are not pale, they feel no pain. However, God can give us wisdom to recognize mental illness. Once, a Christian woman noticed that her husband's attitudes and behaviors had started to change. He was not paying attention to her, was struggling at work, and stopped showing her the affection he used to. This wife prayed for a long time for her husband to change, until one day she asked the Lord in prayer why her husband was acting this way. In prayer, she received the revelation that her husband was suffering from a mental illness, and that all of these were symptoms. Faith in God opened her eyes. She accepted the reality, and was able to seek professional help!

There is not always an answer to the "whys" or "what fors." In Romans 8:28 it says, *"And we know that in all things God works for the good of those who love him, who have been called according to his purpose."* Even when we don't understand everything, we can rest in this truth.

Faith in the loving, faithful, and all-powerful God motivates people to seek prompt and timely help.

"The ability of the human heart to cry out to God without reservation creates the opportunity for a healing relationship between wounded humanity and a loving God."[1]

Faced with the presence of mental illness in a family member, many families close themselves off, hide, and conceal the problem from others. Some feel shame or guilt, while others are overwhelmed. Unfortunately, these feelings only delay seeking professional help.

When Carlos, the youngest son of a Christian family deeply committed to the Lord and the church, experienced his first psychotic episode, his parents decided to hide the situation and keep it private. After repeated absences from church meetings, several people contacted them by phone to see what was going on. The pastor visited their home as well. However, all attempts to find out what was happening were unsuccessful. "We're all fine, there's no problem, thank you for the visit," the parents told their church brothers and sisters. Sadly, hiding the illness, not getting the support of the church family, and not seeking professional help for the illness led Carlos to attempt suicide, resulting in urgent psychiatric hospitalization. It was then that the family fell apart and acknowledged the seriousness of the situation. Then they accepted that their son was suffering from a significant illness. They cried out to God with all their hearts and placed their faith in the only one, the faithful and all-powerful God of love, who could help them. Their faith that God was present in the midst of their pain moved them to seek professional help for their son's health. In addition to that professional help, they also accepted the prayers and support of a congregation that loved them and was concerned for them. To this day, Carlos continues with his psychiatric

1. Brueggemann, W. The Psalms and the Life of Faith: A Suggested Typology of Function, Journal for the Study of the Old Testament, 17 (1980), 3-32

treatment, has a good quality of life, and evangelizes every customer he comes into contact with at work.

Every family with a sick member should open up to the help of others: to professionals in the field and also to those in the family of faith. Burdens are lightened when they are shared, and faith is exercised through communion with one another.

Faith in the loving, faithful, and all-powerful God helps the sick person to understand and accept that God loves them.

The psyche cannot be reconstructed without love. Many people have been raised in harsh environments where they lack love or are rejected. As adults, these people can develop depressive disorders or personality disorders. It is well known that those who did not receive love find it difficult to give it, and may even display distrust when someone expresses love to them. Often, when these types of people receive Christ, they feel overwhelmed by the love of God. This is one of the things that most impacts their lives. They may now be suffering the natural consequences of the sin for which others made them suffer in their childhood. Now they are going through a mental illness, but they can also enjoy having met Jesus Christ as their Savior. They can enjoy His love, and know they have the help of God permanently. Ephesians 3:12 says, *"In him and through faith in him we may approach God with freedom and confidence."* The sick person who has faith in God knows that He is his creator and that He knows him better than anyone.

Although in the darkness of the night of suffering someone who is ill may not see the way out, or feel God's presence by his side, but still that person can cling to the truth of the well-known verse, John 3:16: *"For God so loved the world that he gave his one and only Son, that whoever believes in him shall not perish but have eternal life."* Even in suffering, each of us can accept the gift of God's unconditional love.

In 1 John 4:16 it says, *"And so we know and rely on the love God has for us. God is love. Whoever lives in love lives in God, and God in them."* He who has not felt love in his childhood can feel it as an adult through faith in God, who tells him that He loves him deeply. Now he can love God, and love himself and others!

Faith in the loving, faithful, and all-powerful God helps the sick person to rely on prayer.

Humans have a basic need to be heard and understood. By reducing their social interactions, the mentally ill often have limited opportunities to connect and talk with others—which is problematic, because social contact is crucial for the improvement of their symptoms. Someone with mental illness may also fear not being understood or even being criticized if they share what they are going through. A person of faith knows that God listens and understands. That He will not criticize if they share their frustrations and complaints with Him in prayer. And, unlike people, He is accessible at any time of the day or night.

Many patients with mental illness experience a change in their sleep-wake cycle, sleeping during the day and staying awake at night. In the solitude of the night, they can talk to God knowing that He is not sleeping, that they are not bothering Him, and that He listens to their pleas. Through faith, the sick can seek comfort by pouring out their feelings of pain to the Lord in prayer and finding relief. In Psalm 66:20 we read, *"Praise be to God, who has not rejected my prayer or withheld his love from me."* God gives an attentive ear to our pleas. When praying, the sick person can open their heart, their emotions, and their frustrations, without feeling judged, because they know that God understands them.

Many mental illnesses have a prolonged evolution, and some persist throughout life. In all stages of a mental illness, from the shock when it appears to the resignation when it becomes chronic, constancy in prayer can sustain the person with mental illness. Once, the wife of a pastor who had been dealing with mental illness for many years told me (Daniel) about the medication she had been prescribed. "Doctor, I accept this medication, but I rely on faith," she said. In the book of Psalms, we find prayers from hearts that suffer in difficult and desperate times. Many are sincere laments, raw cries that remind us that packaging pain before God is of little use because He knows everything and is there with the one who suffers.

Psalm 77 is the prayer of a grieving and sorrowful heart, and it describes many of the feelings that arise when a person goes through a time of sadness, pain, or depression. We invite you to read it. This psalm is a prayer that reveals an open heart with complete sincerity before the Lord. Its heartbreaking complaints and raw questions clearly express some of the symptoms of the depressive state of a faithful and sincere child of God. The person clearly accepts their experience and continues to trust in the Lord, recalling from afar His past goodness and mercies.

The faith in the loving, faithful, and all-powerful God helps the sick person to participate in a church and share with others.

Mentally ill patients often lose their sense of belonging in the groups they were once part of. If a teenager used to attend school, maybe they stop going, or their absences extend for long periods. Adults may stop going to work due to illness. They sometimes even stop meeting with friends. For someone with a mental disorder, having faith and belonging to a Christian community can be very helpful.

Mental illness is not contagious, but FAITH is!

Sharing with others promotes health by connecting each person with social, emotional, and spiritual support, mitigating the negative effects of the illness. Mentally ill patients tend to isolate themselves and lose contact with others. Phone calls, visits to their homes, warm greetings, a pat on the back, a smile, a hug, calling them by their name, inviting them to activities, or involving them in a program are all gestures of great help. When the church makes these types of efforts, it can help to grow a therapeutic and loving community for those with mental illness and for others.

Elsa is a Christian woman who suffers from a depressive illness for which she is receiving psychiatric treatment. She finds it difficult to leave her house. She is a member of a church but has been attending infrequently since becoming ill. She knows that prayers are being offered for her at the church's weekly prayer meetings. A sister from the congregation calls her three times a week to pray for her. These brief prayers bring Elsa great comfort, and she eagerly looks forward to these calls. On one occasion, the church pastor and two deacons visited Elsa at her home, prayed for her, and anointed her with oil. In James 5:14-15, it says, *"Is anyone among you sick? Let them call the elders of the church to pray over them and anoint them with oil in the name of the Lord. And the prayer offered in faith will make the sick person well; the Lord will raise them up."* The following Sunday, Elsa attended the church meeting. She looked better, and from that moment on, she had a healthier attitude toward life.

We know that mental illness is not contagious, but faith is! Spending time in the company of others who have faith can influence the mind and emotions of someone with mental illness, helping them to live with constant trust in God. Faith and a sense of trust are transmitted through speech. When a person with mental illness hears other Christians share their faith, it can become ingrained in their mind and may help them continue to trust in God.

Faith in the loving, faithful, and all-powerful God brings peace.

Some time ago, I received an advertisement from a cruise line that promotes its trips with the slogan "Peace of Mind." This well-thought-out slogan encourages customers to travel peacefully, with peace, because the cruise company will take care of all the details. Isn't this what the Lord wants to do with all troubled people? Does He not want to give each of us peace of mind? All believers know this, but sometimes it seems not enough when illness arises. It was not enough for the disciples who were in the boat with Jesus in the midst of the storm. There, the Lord's question to them was, "Why are you afraid?" And it was not enough for Peter when, while walking on water, he stopped looking at Jesus. Then the question was, "Peter, why did you doubt?"

Doubts and fears can take away peace. In these circumstances, the prayer should be, "Lord, increase our faith!" Putting trust and faith in God brings true peace in the midst of mental illness, either one's own or that of a friend or family member. We read in John 14:27, *"Peace I leave with you; my peace I give you. I do not give to you as the world gives. Do not let your hearts be troubled and do not be afraid."* Many mentally ill people have become dependent on anxiolytics and tranquilizers and they may self-medicate, increasing the dosage to find some relief from their symptoms. They carry their medications everywhere—in their purse, in their pocket, in the glove compartment of the car—and become distressed when they don't have them. The true promise is that the Lord is the one who gives peace. Medications can be used as directed by the doctor, but should not be depended on.

Some sick people, unable to sleep and remaining awake for a long time at night, experience fears, restlessness, and lack of calm. In these cases, remembering verses such as Psalm 4:8 *("In peace I will lie down and sleep, for you alone, Lord, make me dwell in safety")* or

Proverbs 3:24 *("When you lie down, you will not be afraid, you will lie down and your sleep will be sweet")* can help a lot. Having faith in what the Bible says helps the sick person to relax and sleep peacefully.

Faith in the loving and all-powerful God helps the sick person to know and trust in God's promises.

When a person accepts Christ as their Savior, they receive eternal life, the Holy Spirit, and an inheritance that they will not only enjoy in heaven, but also on this earth. They become heirs to the promises that He left in His Word! Galatians 3:29 says, *"And if you belong to Christ, then you are Abraham's seed, and heirs according to the promise God made."* The sick person who trusts in God, knows His promises and trusts in them, can rely on those promises to sustain them in their daily lives.

Although questions don't always have answers, it is always good to declare the promises of God, remembering that He is our peace, our strong tower, our rock, and our help in times of trouble, and that Jesus said that He would be with us every day until the end of the world.

The person of faith knows the promises, keeps them in their mind and heart, and trusts in them because they know they are true, because God is faithful! Faith in a faithful and true God invigorates and strengthens the sick. Faith gives them confidence and certainty to keep going despite the difficult circumstances they may face.

One suggestion we can give to those suffering from any kind of illness is to write in a notebook all the promises they find while reading the Bible. Then, by reading that list periodically, those promises can help to increase their faith (if possible, it can be helpful to write the promises in the first person, and claim them for one's own life with faith).

Some beautiful promises from God's Word that can help those who are mentally ill are:

> *"The Lord is faithful, and he will strengthen you..."* (2 Thessalonians 3:3). *(First person example: "The Lord is faithful, and he will strengthen me.")*
>
> *"Know therefore that the Lord your God is God, the faithful God who keeps his gracious covenant loyalty for a thousand generations with those who love him and keep his commandments"* (Deuteronomy 7:9).
>
> *"The one who calls you is faithful, and he will do it"* (1 Thessalonians 5:24).
>
> *"Let us hold unswervingly to the hope we profess, for he who promised is faithful"* (Hebrews 10:23).
>
> *"The Lord will keep you from all harm—he will watch over your life; the Lord will watch over your coming and going both now and forevermore"* (Psalm 121:7-8, NIV).

The mentally ill who have faith live with confidence.

The person who has faith trusts that God, with His love, will always care for and protect them, because they trust in His promises. The mentally ill person who has faith lives with confidence. God's faithfulness is forever!

Faith in the loving, faithful, and all-powerful God brings hope.

Hope is the confidence of achieving something or of something desired coming true. The hope of the mentally ill person who relies on God is certainty, expectation, and conviction that God has control over their illness. This brings someone suffering peace and security, helping them to live day by day. Hope protects the mind from fear, distress, and negative and catastrophic thoughts. Romans 12:12 says,

"Be joyful in hope, patient in affliction, faithful in prayer." Hope in the Lord brings joy and dispels sadness. It provides security, confidence, and certainty. Hope conquers despair, which is so common in the mentally ill and their families. Faith gives hope, and putting hope in God frees from anguish and anxiety.

In the Word of God, we find three images about hope. It is represented as a helmet, an anchor, and a gateway.

7. **Helmet:** Hope is a helmet that covers the mind from doubts and negative, catastrophic, and destructive thoughts. In 1 Thessalonians 5:8 we read, *"But let us, who are of the day, be sober, putting on the breastplate of faith and love; and for a helmet, the hope of salvation."*
8. **Anchor:** Hope is an anchor that keeps the ill secure and firm in God when going through the storms of mental illness. We read in Hebrews 6:19, *"We have this hope as an anchor for the soul, firm and secure. It enters the inner sanctuary behind the curtain."* In Christian catacombs, Jews had the symbol of the anchor next to the cross, speaking of hope in Christ. When emotions are about to sink the ill into despair and sadness, hope that springs from faith lifts them up and helps them feel the presence of a sustaining God. Faith is an anchor that provides security in the midst of illness.
9. **Gateway:** Hope is a gateway to the reality that, even while living with illness, the Lord can help the ill have a good quality of life. In Hosea 2:15 we read, *"There I will give her back her vineyards, and will make the Valley of Achor a door of hope."* Hope helps the ill and their families to see their situation from a different perspective. It is possible to get out of the confinement of depression or other mental illness through the gate of hope, trusting that Christ has plans and purposes for each person's life.

The joy and peace of the soul are related to hope. *"May the God of hope fill you with all joy and peace as you trust in him, so that you may overflow with hope by the power of the Holy Spirit"* (Romans 15:13, NIV).

Chapter 4

Brief description of mental illnesses

The objectives of this chapter are:

- To become acquainted with these illnesses, as not knowing them may lead to misidentification or misinterpretation.
- To be able to detect mental illnesses (the earlier, the better).
- To be aware that they can occur in members of the church or family.
- To avoid mistaking or labeling those who suffer from mental illness, wrongly thinking that "the problem is spiritual."
- To gain better understanding in order to help those who are going through any of these illnesses.

1. Mood Disorders

Mood disorders are mental disorders whose main characteristic is the alteration of the individual's mood. They are also known as affective disorders. Changes in mood are intense enough to affect daily life in terms of work, education, personal relationships, and even service to God. The most common mood disorders are depression and bipolar disorder.

Depression

Depression is an illness (sometimes severe) with multiple clinical forms, and can be linked to many factors. Depression can be a way to defend oneself from extreme psychological suffering. Sometimes it occurs without a known cause.

Depression can deteriorate many important aspects of a person's life, including their desire to live and their vitality. A very common expression in depressed individuals is, "I don't feel like..." They lack the inner strength to carry out the tasks they always did. For instance, "I don't feel like praising, going to church, or praying..." If this happens in the context of depression, we should not judge the person as if they were "spiritually tepid," but rather consider that they are going through an illness that requires professional attention. Thanks to the advances in medicine, there are now treatments for depression that alleviate symptoms or cure it completely.

Depression presents many symptoms. The most distinctive is sadness. This feeling oscillates between deep sadness and intense hopelessness, to the point of no longer wanting to live or wanting to die. Although we all feel down or sad at some points, when these feelings persist for a prolonged period, it a sign of a mental disorder that can be very serious and debilitating for the individual.

The depressive person typically isolates themselves, seeking to be alone. They typically avoid friends and family and become more and more separate from social life. This is what is called hibernation: many people stay in bed without the desire to get up. For others, daily commitments are difficult to face. Everything seems too heavy. They feel too weak, and many say, "I don't have the strength to face the world." This makes the person with depression lose contact with the world and with themselves.

There are different types of depression:

- Major depressive disorder (often simply called "depression").
- Persistent depressive disorder (dysthymia).
- Premenstrual dysphoric disorder (severe depressive symptoms and anxiety that occur in women before menstruation).
- Depressive disorder due to another illness (for example, cancer).
- Substance or medication-induced depressive disorder.
- Melancholia.
- Reactive depression.
- Seasonal depression (seasonal affective disorder).

Bipolar disorder

Bipolar disorder is an illness that, without treatment, can lead to suicide. It is an increasingly common mental disorder, characterized by exaggerated changes in mood ranging from depression to mania. Mania is a state of abnormally elevated, euphoric, expansive mood, where the person is hyperactive, irritable, and sleeps little. This affects how the person acts, thinks, and feels. Bipolar disorder cycles last for days, weeks, or months and can seriously impair the person's work and social relationships.

During manic episodes, the person may even stop working or following schedules and norms. They may engage in unproductive activities, increase their debts through compulsive spending, and feel full of energy even with little sleep, potentially appearing irritable and prone to arguments. During depressive episodes, the patient commonly does not even want to get out of bed. Since it is important to stabilize the patient's mood, it is necessary to consult a professional because bipolar disorder requires treatment and psychiatric medication.

2. Anxiety Disorders

The terms distress, nervousness, insecurity, restlessness, tension, fear, or dread are descriptions of different experiences related to anxiety. Anxiety disorders are conditions in which these symptoms do not disappear and may worsen over time.

The symptoms of anxiety disorders can interfere with daily activities, such as ministry in the church, work performance, school, and relationships. Anxiety disorders can alter the course of thought, making one's perspective less objective, which leads to categorizing things in a pessimistic and catastrophic way. Anxiety disorders seriously limit a person's ability to focus and concentrate because the mind is occupied by many ideas of suffering. The person suffering from anxiety is not always understood by those around them.

Anxiety disorders can manifest in different forms. The most common types of anxiety are:

Panic Disorder

When anxiety is very severe and acute, it can paralyze the individual, turning into panic. Panic is an extreme response to a case of anxiety. It is an experience of intense fear, with a feeling of loss of control, fainting, or fear of imminent death. These symptoms are part of the crisis called a "panic attack" that occurs suddenly in predisposed individuals. The duration of a panic attack can vary from a few minutes to several hours.

Example of a case of panic disorder: Javier is a young adult who has a long medical history of clinical, cardiological, and neurological studies. All these studies aimed to diagnose why symptoms appeared suddenly when he was on his way to work or to a group activity with his friends, without any other trigger. In these times he experienced shortness of breath, palpitations, sweating, and the fear that he could die at that moment. All the results of the analysis and studies were normal, but Javier continued having these episodes. In his church congregation, Javier's leader told him that his lack of faith in God was causing these fears (it goes without saying that questioning his lack of faith generated more anguish and worsened his condition).

Phobia

Phobia is a persistent, excessive, irrational, and disproportionate fear of certain objects, animals, or situations, accompanied by a marked tendency to avoid them. Phobias can cause great discomfort or suffering and significant restrictions in daily life, whether in interpersonal, work, or family relationships. There may be fears of abandonment, rejection, criticism, failure, the unknown, one's own death, the death of loved ones, etc.

There are three main categories of phobic anxiety disorders: agoraphobia (fear of being alone and of public places), social phobia (shyness and anxiety in front of others with whom one has to interact), and specific phobias, such as arachnophobia (fear of spiders). Specific phobias can relate to things or events that cause extreme fear, such as specific objects or specific situations. For example, someone may be afraid of storms, birds, snakes, or flying on a plane. Specific phobias are easier for most people to understand than other types.

Obsessive-Compulsive Disorder

Obsessions refers to inappropriate and dominant thoughts or images that are repeatedly present in a person's mind and that cause distress.

Sometimes the person may recognize that these concerns are not real, but they still feel helpless to make any decision about them or to suppress or ignore these unpleasant thoughts or images.

Compulsions are repeated actions carried out as a result of these thoughts or images. Those who suffer from this disorder feel that they have to control (or re-control) how certain actions are carried out, or they may feel the need to carry out certain tasks in the form of a ritual. If they fail to perform these behaviors, their anxiety grows. Some examples of compulsions are repeated hand washing; repeated smoothing of bedspreads, pillows, curtains, or towels; checking that certain tasks have been carried out correctly or that certain objects have been arranged in a certain way; and hoarding, which refers to the inability to throw anything away.

People with obsessive compulsive disorder can have disturbing thoughts about God and their salvation, a spiritual if not neurotic product. Being able to explain this to someone suffering often helps to calm them down, reducing their anxiety.

Example of a case of obsessive compulsion: a very committed young Christian suddenly has pervasive thoughts that he considers sinful and even blasphemous. This distresses him greatly and he repeats long prayers several times a day asking for forgiveness. These thoughts only calm down during sleep. In an attempt to alleviate these thoughts, this young man increases how much time he spends, isolating himself from his daily activities. At the same time, he has a great fear of losing the salvation of his soul.

Post-Traumatic Stress Disorder

Traumatic experiences that lead to post-traumatic stress disorder include natural disasters (such as earthquakes, cyclones, hurricanes, and floods), wars, robberies, transportation accidents, domestic violence, suicide of family members, friends, or colleagues, physical or sexual abuse, severe life-threatening illnesses, or the loss of loved ones. In all these cases, the disorder occurs when individuals have experienced the trauma personally or have witnessed it. People suffering from post-traumatic stress disorder live in a constant state of fear and repeatedly relive their experience in their thoughts, dreams (with nightmares that recall the lived experience), drawings, speech, and relationships with others. They are constantly on edge and fear that something bad will happen or that the traumatic event will recur, repeatedly recalling the experience. They may have trouble falling asleep or staying asleep, be irritable, have outbursts of anger, have trouble concentrating, always be on alert (a state called hypervigilance), or exhibit an exaggerated defensive reflexes (such as jumping with their entire body when confronted with an unfamiliar noise).

An example case of post-traumatic stress disorder: A young man was robbed at gunpoint. When he got off the bus, his backpack with his computer, containing part of a research paper for his graduation, was taken from him. There was a struggle and screaming, and a bullet that was fired but missed him. The young man's helplessness and despair resulted in post-traumatic stress disorder with all its characteristic symptoms. Months later, he still suffered instant, involuntary memories of the episode at random throughout the day, and experiences extreme anxiety when approached by a stranger or when passing through a place that reminds him of the scene.

Social Anxiety Disorder

People with social anxiety disorder do not commonly seek help because those who suffer from it believe it is just the way they are. These people tend not to associate social anxiety disorder with an emotional problem, except when it is accompanied with depression or panic attacks. Social anxiety disorder is difficult to diagnose. It sometimes manifests as extreme shyness in social situations, distress, and fear of ridicule or humiliating situations. In other cases, it is characterized by symptoms such as feeling embarrassment and blushing when having to speak in a social group; by intense and irrational fear that causes dizziness, nausea, or stomach pain in new situations; by intense anxiety or even anguish during a job interview or when being observed eating, performing, or speaking in front of friends or strangers.

An example case of social anxiety: a 10-year-old girl sporadically experienced stomach pain and the desire to use the bathroom before going to school. She said she didn't feel well and didn't want to go to school. These episodes occurred when she knew she would have to speak in front of her classmates that day. Simply the thought of having to speak in front of others, being looked at, heard, and possibly judged caused her a great deal of anxiety. She was labeled as introverted, solitary, and antisocial. Because the adults in her life didn't realize that she was suffering from social anxiety, she did not receive appropriate help.

Generalized Anxiety Disorder

Worrying about things is normal, but it becomes problematic when worry occurs so constantly that it interferes with the person's life.

Worrying about things is normal, but it's not normal when worry occurs so constantly that it interferes with a person's life. People with this disorder often worry about everything: studies, work, relationships, church, leaving the house and the possibility of getting into an accident, etc.

Generalized anxiety disorder represents more than 50% of all anxiety disorders and is the second most common mental disorder after depression. Women are twice as likely as men to suffer from generalized anxiety disorder. The predominant symptoms vary, with the most frequent being constantly feeling nervous, trembling, muscle tension, sweating, dizziness, palpitations, vertigo, and epigastric discomfort.

3. Psychological Disorders

Psychotic disorders are serious. When suffering from a psychological disorder, a person loses touch with reality and may experience hallucinations and delusions.

Psychotic disorders are characterized by the impairment of dopaminergic and glutamatergic neurotransmission in the hippocampus, midbrain, striatum, and prefrontal cortex. They are due to a neurodevelopmental issues, and according to findings in epidemiological studies, heredity is a factor in the pathophysiology of many psychoses.

Psychotic disorders include delusional disorders or paranoia (where the person is totally convinced of things that are not true) and schizophrenia (where the person experiences hallucinations or disturbing thoughts). Schizophrenia strikes young people. Almost 90% develop symptoms between the ages of 15 and 40. Schizophrenia affects about 1% of the world population and occurs equally among men and women. It is a serious brain disorder that prevents people from differentiating between real and unreal experiences, thinking logically, or having normal emotional responses to social situations. It is often a frightening and difficult-to-understand illness, especially when symptoms first appear and in the early days after diagnosis. The initial symptoms can cause alarm or fear, especially if they are considered to be the result of demonic or satanic activity.

The symptoms of the schizophrenia are usually difficult to detect at first. Schizophrenics often feel tense, have trouble sleeping or concentrating, isolate themselves, and lose friendships. As the disease progresses, psychotic symptoms such as delusions, beliefs, or groundless thoughts develop; people with schizophrenia experience hallucinations (hearing or feeling things that are not present), strange or incomprehensible behaviors unrelated to the environment, or suffer from blunting of affect, meaning they do not show any emotion.

The earlier schizophrenia is recognized and diagnosed, the better. An early diagnosis leads to early treatment and increases the chances of a quick recovery.

Here are five tips to keep in mind if you ever find yourself with someone with psychosis who is telling you about their delusions and hallucinations:

1. Stay calm, relaxed, warm, and optimistic. Never show anxiety or concern. Take what they are telling you as natural, because a person with psychosis is very vulnerable to stress and very perceptive of the fear or insecurity of other people. Instill hope for the future.
2. When you say something, your emotional tone should be calm. Speak in a low volume. For instance, if you want to show love or concern regarding something the person with psychosis is doing, or joy at being able to talk to them, be careful not to be too expressive.
3. Avoid stressful situations. If you notice the person getting tense about something, quickly change the subject.
4. Maintain a linear dialogue. Convey only one concept at a time. Do not indicate several things at the same time, such as, "It's a good idea to read the Bible because it would help you, and pray every day when you wake up." It would be better to say, "Reading the Bible would be good for you," and wait for their response. In the case of a patient who spends a lot of time in bed, a non-linear

dialogue would be "Get up because it's a beautiful day. I've prepared a nice breakfast and we need to go out soon." That combines too many future actions and logical connections. It would be better to say, "It's time to get up," see how the person responds, then continue with the next thing to do.

5. Social contacts decrease or disappear for those with psychosis, so it's very important to encourage relationships. Whenever it is possible and beneficial, it can be good for people with psychosis to stay in contact with people from their church congregations.

Family relationships are key to the patient's stability.

What can you do as a leader or pastor for the family of a person with schizophrenia? If you find yourself in contact with relatives of a person suffering from schizophrenia, remember that family relationships are key to the patient's stability.

Here are some tips:

- Create a warm and tolerant atmosphere for the person with psychosis's family members in the church, and encourage them to do the same for the patient at home.
- Remove any burden family members of a person with psychosis may feel from shame or guilt (both are unjustified, but they may still feel them).
- Help the family of a person with psychosis provide love and unconditional support to the patient.
- Ensure that the family members their daily routine as much as possible.
- Advise family members to comply with the treatment, as the risk associated with non-compliance is very high (the patient is five times more likely to have relapses).

Good outcomes for patients with psychosis often depend on a favorable family environment that lovingly accepts the person with their illness.

4. Personality disorders

Personality is a set of characteristics or patterns that define a person by their feelings, thoughts, attitudes, and behavior. Each person is born with their personality to some extent because it is conditioned by biology, but the personality will change and develop over time based on each person's relationships with the environment. People with a personality disorder have emotions, behaviors, and impulses that are very different from what would be expected of them. These maladjustments may have caused them concern, misunderstanding, rejection, or anger. People with a personality disorder do not change their behavior to adjust to social norms; they live as if their way of being is normal. They tend to be inflexible, even when confronted with what they are doing or when their behaviors are repeatedly ineffective and have negative consequences. They believe that there is nothing to reproach about what they are doing, and deny their problems or the problems they cause. They typically do not accept counseling or psychological treatment. Generally, people with a personality disorder have decreased introspection, meaning that they do not question themselves. They are unable to reflect on their behavior or emotions.

The person does not present any physical illness that justifies their particular way of being. Personality disorders result from the interaction between genes and the environment. That is, some people are born with a genetic tendency to suffer from a personality disorder, and this tendency decreases or increases depending on environmental factors. Generally, genes and the environment contribute equally to the development of personality disorders, which usually begin in adolescence.

Psychiatry manuals mention ten different types of personality disorders. We have divided them here into four broad groups:

1. One group is characterized by eccentric or strange thoughts or behaviors. These are people who are distrustful, always suspecting others (for example, a person who unjustifiably and consistently suspects that their spouse is being unfaithful). They believe that others are trying to deceive or harm them. Innocent comments are taken as aggressive, double-edged, or personal attacks, and they react with anger or rage. In general, these people prefer to be alone.
2. Another group of people show indifference to the needs or feelings of others. They behave aggressively or violently in interpersonal relationships, argue with other drivers while in traffic, and are belligerent, impulsive, and irresponsible. They lack remorse for their behavior, lie frequently, and have a history engaging in scams. Some may even act maliciously.
3. In a third group are people who constantly seek attention, have shallow and changing emotions, and are excessively concerned with their physical appearance. They feel special. They fantasize about power, success, and attractiveness. They exaggerate their achievements and are arrogant.
4. A fourth group shows excessive sensitivity to criticism or rejection. They feel inferior and have very low self-esteem. They can tolerate abusive or inadequate treatment. They are inhibited, submissive, shy, socially isolated, and have difficulty expressing disagreement with others in a group. They are afraid of disapproval, embarrassment, or ridicule. They have difficulty initiating and carrying out projects due to lack of self-confidence.

5. Neurocognitive disorders

Neurocognitive disorders consist of alterations in cognitive abilities, such as memory, perception, and problem-solving. It is important to clarify that although cognitive disorders are present in many mental disorders (such as schizophrenia or bipolar disorders), only those disorders whose basic characteristics are cognitive are included in the neurocognitive disorders.

Neurocognitive disorders occur most often in older adults (the likelihood of developing a cognitive disorder increases after the age of 60), but can also affect younger individuals. It is important to understand that neurocognitive disorders involve a deterioration in cognition, meaning a decrease below the level of functioning that was previously normal for that person. Reduced cognitive capacity can include problems with learning and memory, complex attention, executive functioning, expressive and receptive language, and perceptual and motor skills. These symptoms can be caused by a neurodegenerative condition such as Alzheimer's disease, by other illnesses such as Parkinson's disease or Huntington's disease, or by a stroke or traumatic brain injury. They can also develop as a result of substance abuse. All of this leads to changes in behavior and difficulties in carrying out daily tasks.

6. Neurological Diseases

Epilepsy

Epilepsy is a very common disease of the nervous system, generated by the irritation of neurons. The main symptom of this irritation is involuntary body movements, which occur unexpectedly. Some of these involuntary movements are generalized (seizures), and others partial, with movements of a part of the body or "absences." An absence is a loss of consciousness in which the person stares blankly and lost for a few seconds. The person is not aware of this, and after the seizure, they continue with their activity without remembering anything about it. Six out of every thousand people in the world have epilepsy, and it influences the cognition, emotions, and social relationships of the person who suffers from it. Fortunately, there are numerous medications available today to alleviate these symptoms.

It is important to remember that you should seek help if you are with a person who has a convulsive seizure that lasts more than five minutes or if a series of seizures occurs without the person regaining consciousness between them, as well as if the person is injured during the seizure.

Other neurological diseases include multiple sclerosis, Parkinson's disease, and dementia, which we will explain below.

Dementia

Dementia is a serious and progressive mental illness characterized by the loss or weakening of mental faculties, with memory and reasoning impairment often accompanied by behavioral disorders. Dementia (caused by aging of the brain with the death of neurons and their connections) is among the most prevalent conditions of old age. The most common form of dementia is Alzheimer's disease, which is the severe and progressive deterioration of mental capacity that interferes with the person's daily life.

An elderly person with no activity who is confined to their home has a higher likelihood of getting sick.

Some symptoms of Alzheimer's include loss of memory (especially recent memory, which is generally noticed by people who spend time with a person with Alzheimer's), difficulty in communicating or finding words to mention objects or activities, getting lost while driving or walking, and difficulty in performing tasks that were previously capable of, such as paying taxes or cooking. In addition to cognitive disorders, behavior disorders can also result, such as insomnia, depression, anxiety, agitation, hallucinations, shouting, persecutory ideas (I'm being robbed, I'm being kidnapped), or aggression. All behavioral disorders are treatable, unlike cognitive deterioration. There are currently few therapeutic resources to prevent the progression of this disease.

If a family member, fellow Christian, or friend suffers from dementia, it is important to keep in mind some advice:

- Evaluate their social environment. Many adults find themselves alone, without close ties. Try to provide them with the necessary company and assistance.
- Evaluate their level of activity. An older adult without activity and confined to their home is more likely to become ill. Organize special activities for this group within your congregation.
- Evaluate their need for help. Check whether the person can handle basic daily tasks (buying medication and food; walking and transportation; hygiene and household care) and help them get any necessary assistance.

There are many prejudices about old age. As Christians, we must value this stage of life as the Bible teaches us:

> *"Gray hair is a crown of glory; it is gained in a righteous life."* (Proverbs 16:31)
>
> *"They still bear fruit in old age; they are ever full of sap and green."* (Psalms 92:14)
>
> *"The glory of young men is their strength, gray hair the splendor of the old."* (Proverbs 20:29)

> *"You shall stand up before the gray head and honor the face of an old man, and you shall fear your God: I am the Lord."* (Leviticus 19:32)

The elderly in the Bible are associated with glory, honor, beauty, fruit, knowledge, wisdom, and respect. Let's learn to take care of them as they deserve!

Asperger's

Asperger's syndrome was first described in 1944 by the Austrian pediatrician Hans Asperger, based on his observation of a group of children characterized by being socially strange, naïve, disconnected from each other, having good grammar and extensive vocabulary, and speaking fluently but literally. These children had poor non-verbal communication, poor motor coordination, and a lack of common sense, interested in specific topics, and with average or above average intelligence but difficulty in learning conventional tasks. Asperger's causes significant disability in social, occupational, and other important areas of development.

On the other hand, individuals with Asperger's may also have an extensive vocabulary, good memory capacity, skill with processing visual information, and a keen perception of details that may go unnoticed by others. They also tend to be very responsible, noble, and loyal individuals. This syndrome is a neurodevelopmental disorder that is part of the autism spectrum disorders (ASD) and affects the person primarily in three areas.:

1. Difficulty in social interaction, manifested as at least two of the following: eye contact, facial expression, or body postures. This difficulty is not always due to lack of interest, but rather lack of skills. These individuals also display the absence of emotional reciprocity.

2. Restricted patterns of behavior, interests, and activities, and high cognitive and behavioral rigidity. Repetitive behaviors. Absorbing preoccupation, limited to certain topics of interest, which is abnormal in its intensity and focus.
3. Hyper or hypoactivity in response to certain sensory stimuli. That is, excessive sensitivity to certain sounds or smells, and decreased sensitivity to pain or temperature.

Asperger's syndrome may be attributed to a combination of genetic and environmental factors that impact brain development. This type of autism tends to run in families, suggesting that some cases may be hereditary.

This syndrome usually does not involve cognitive delay, neither in language acquisition nor in development. There are no valid biological markers. The diagnosis is based on a behavioral analysis, and individuals with the disorder display diverse behaviors and symptoms. An early diagnosis is essential to work with the child on these difficulties, as well as to provide guidance for the family and teachers to help with the individual's development and facilitate their social inclusion.

7. Eating Disorders

Anorexia Nervosa

Those who suffer from anorexia nervosa have a distorted and delusional perception of their own body, causing the patient to see themselves as fat, even when their weight is below the recommended range. As a result, the person obsessively controls the amount of food eaten, restricts intake, diets and fasts, takes laxatives and diuretics, and exercises excessively.

In anorexia nervosa, the patient fears gaining weight. Therefore, the patient initiates a gradual decrease in weight by depriving themselves of certain high-calorie foods and reducing overall food intake. This can lead to physical health problems such as anemia, fatigue, insomnia, dizziness or fainting, bluish discoloration of the fingers, thin or brittle hair, loss of hair, the growth of downy body hair, absence of menstruation, constipation and abdominal pain, dry or yellowish skin, intolerance to cold, irregular heartbeat, low blood pressure, dehydration, and swelling of the arms or legs due to fluid accumulation from renal dysfunction.

Due to its characteristics and severity, this disease requires a multidisciplinary approach:

- Clinical doctor (for all physical disorders, which may even require hospitalization).
- Psychiatrist (for the need for medication due to the distorted and delusional perception of the body).
- Psychologist (for the emotional self-esteem disorder).
- Nutritionist (to indicate a specific diet appropriate for each patient).
- Family counseling (to achieve awareness within the family and cooperation in treatment).

Bulimia Nervosa

Bulimia is a disease characterized by abnormal patterns of eating, with some episodes of massive intake of food, and others of elimination of those calories through vomiting or laxatives. Its essential characteristic is that the person suffers episodes of compulsive overeating followed by a great feeling of guilt and loss of control. This is usually alternated with episodes of fasting or very little food intake, but the person soon suffers from episodes of compulsive eating again. The therapeutic approach should be multidisciplinary, as in the case of anorexia.

Binge Eating Disorder

This is a serious disease characterized by the person consuming large amounts of food and feeling like they are losing control while eating. Severe distress follows the binge due to the potential weight gain.

All of these eating disorders have something in common: a severe disturbance in people's eating behaviors, and the thoughts and emotions related to eating and body image.

It is a good idea for leaders and pastors to address following concepts in our groups of adolescents and young people:

- Questioning the cult of beauty and external image, so prevalent in today's culture.
- Improving self-esteem. Helping people feel good about themselves, with who they are and how they are.
- Encouraging exercises such as smiling in front of the mirror, learning to look at themselves in a different way, highlighting inner beauty.
- Confronting thoughts and values that make them believe that their image is more important than their person.
- Teaching them to see themselves through spiritual values so that they can see themselves as God sees them: unique, valuable, and loved.

Chapter 5

Renowned people with mental illness

Those suffering from some kind of illness, deficiency, or mental disability can develop their gifts and serve others. Any Christian can fulfill God's purpose for their life even in the midst of illness or suffering, because God is perfected in our weaknesses. God cares about the faithfulness of the Christian, not their health.

People with mental illnesses should not be defined by it. They are simply going through a mental illness.

People with mental illnesses should not be defined by it. They are simply going through a mental illness. Illness does not limit their identity or value, but only affects some function or performance; they still retain most of their abilities, capacities, and wit.

We will mention some examples of people who excelled in their field of work while experiencing mental illness. These people's mental illness did not limit them in the development of talents and gifts.

Charles Spurgeon (pastor, preacher, and writer)

Charles Spurgeon suffered from depression. Despite this suffering, due to his faith, loyalty, and love for the Lord, he became considered one of the greatest preachers in history and was called "the prince of preachers."

Spurgeon was born in England in 1834. In London, he led the largest congregation of the time with 5,600 seats. His sermons were published in newspapers including the London *Times and the New York Times*. His sermons, compiled during his ministry at the Metropolitan Tabernacle, fill 63 volumes. Spurgeon said that in prayer lay the power of the church, and during his sermons, he would gather some brothers in an adjoining room to intercede during his preaching.

1858, he suffered an episode that kept him away from the pulpit for three Sundays; upon his return, his message was about 1 Peter 1:6-7, which says, *"In all this you greatly rejoice, though now for a little while you may have had to suffer grief in all kinds of trials. These have come so that the proven genuineness of your faith—of greater worth than gold, which perishes even though refined by fire—may result in praise, glory and honor when Jesus Christ is revealed."*

On another occasion, Spurgeon wrote to his congregation at the Metropolitan Tabernacle, "Dear friends, the furnace is burning higher around me. Since I last preached to you, I have been cast down very low, my body tortured with much pain, and my spirit prostrated with depression."[1]

---

1. Spurgeon y sus aflicciones. (Spurgeon and his woes) - allanroman.blogspot.com https://bit.ly/30N7 8wp

Spurgeon found consolation in his suffering, recognizing that depression equipped him to minister with greater power and effectiveness. On one occasion, he said, "I would go to the deeps a hundred times to cheer a downcast spirit. It is good for me to have been afflicted, that I might know how to speak a word in season to one that is weary."

In a sermon titled "The Affliction and the Joy of the Christian," he referred to his illness, saying, "My spirit was so low, that I could weep for hours like a child, and yet I knew not what I wept for."

On one occasion, this faithful, faith-filled Christian expressed the following: "A good friend was telling me about a poor woman who was suffering great pain but was full of joy and gladness; hearing this story made me feel very distressed and ashamed of myself." Due to his mental illness, Spurgeon often wavered between depression and joy, and he expressed, "That text shone into my soul with real significance, that sometimes the Christian can't bear his sorrows with a brave and joyful heart; sometimes the spirit sinks within him, and the Christian must become like a child smitten by the hand of God." On another occasion, he said, "The mind can descend far lower than the body, because in it there are bottomless pits. The flesh can only bear a certain number of wounds and no more, but the soul can bleed in ten thousand ways and die over and over again every hour."

Any of us could wonder whether it is right for a Christian of Spurgeon's stature to question why he is suffering, yet we know he did, as we read in his writing "The Sword and the Trowel" from 1876. After being limited for a time by his depressive episodes, he posed the question in an article titled "Incapacitated: Why?" There Spurgeon answered his own question, concluding that such times are "the surest means of teaching us that we are not necessary for God's work, and that when we are most useless, He can easily do without us."

Charles Spurgeon is an excellent example of how a Christian can be useful in God's hands even without good mental health. A true example of mental illness and faith, he is someone who showed acceptance of his illness, which without being concealed was used for the glory of God. Spurgeon is an excellent example of serving the Lord despite suffering.[2]

John Bunyan (pastor and writer)

Born in 1628 in England, Bunyan was a prolific English writer and Christian preacher. He was imprisoned from 1660 to 1672 for continuing to preach outside the liturgy imposed by the Anglican Church, which was supposed to be administered only by someone with episcopal orders. During his imprisonment, he wrote his autobiography, Grace Abounding to the Chief of Sinners. In 1675, Bunyan was imprisoned again for six months for refusing to stop preaching, and it was probably during this time that he wrote his famous book The Pilgrim's Progress ("El progreso del peregrino").[3]

In his autobiographical book, he describes in great detail a number of symptoms he suffered, such as sudden vacillations between of hope and fear, threatening doubts about the truths of faith, self-referential interpretations of certain biblical texts, and temptations that did not yield to repeated prayers for forgiveness. These symptoms collectively constitute the mental illness called obsessive compulsive disorder. In his autobiography he wrote, "The tempter came to me again, and this time with a more painful and threatening temptation than before. The temptation was: 'Where is the blessed Christ, exchange him for things of this life, exchange him for something else.' The temptation pursued me for almost a year and it did so continuously that I could not rid myself of it even for a day, not even an hour,

---

2. La angustia y agonía de Charles Spurgeon (the anguish and agony of Charles Spurgeon- http://www.spurgeon.com.mx/angustias.html

3. Bunyan, John. El Progreso del Peregrino (The Pilgrim's Progress). 2009, Editorial CLIE

unless I was asleep. But not even the disgust that the thought produced in me nor the will to resist could diminish its force. The thought always appeared mixed with all the others, so that I could not even eat my food, chop wood, or look away without the temptation being with me. 'Sell Christ for this, sell Christ for that, sell him.' Sometimes it penetrated my thoughts at least a hundred times at once. 'Sell him, sell him.' Sometimes I have tried to fight against these and I have used some of the blessed Paul's sentences against them, but there is nothing to be done; quickly, when I made this kind of argumentation, the thoughts came back again."

In another passage from his autobiography, Bunyan exemplifies his compulsions (a symptom of obsessive compulsive disorder):

> *One day I was between Elstow and Belford, and the temptation fell upon me to test if I had faith by performing a miracle; the miracle I had to perform was to say to the puddles that were in the road 'Dry up!' and to the dry places 'Change into puddles!' And indeed I was about to do it, but just when I was about to say it, another thought came: 'Kneel under that fence and pray first. God will make you capable.' When I did this, the thought came again that if I had prayed and nothing happened, it meant that I had no faith and that I was a reprobate and lost. So I continued for a long time, and I thought that if only those who could do wonderful things could have faith, I must conclude that for the time being I neither had it nor would I have it in the future. So I was again between evil and my own ignorance and was so perplexed that I did not know what to do.*
>
> *These ideas, along with others that right now I do not dare to say either by word or in writing, produced such a convulsion in my spirit and so burdened my heart with their quantity, continuity, and strength that I felt as if there was nothing else within me*

> *from morning to night, as if indeed there could be no space for anything else.4*

This disease did not limit Bunyan; rather, it enabled him to write his famous novel *The Pilgrim's Progress*, a book reprinted to this day and which has been the salvation vehicle for thousands of people. This book is an allegory of the pilgrimage of a soul in search of its eternal salvation, a pilgrim who is constantly besieged by doubt about which path to take, by the despair of uncertainty, and by faith to continue to the celestial city. It is one of the most translated books of English literature, an instrument for many to know Christ as Savior, and the most read book after the Bible in England in its time. In the last years of his life, Bunyan was a Puritan clergyman and was recognized as one of the most important writers of the time.

The following passage, taken from *The Pilgrim's Progress*, shows with masterful literary beauty aspects of Bunyan's own spiritual and emotional struggle:

> *Christian then drew his sword, for he saw that it was time to fight, and Apollyon launched at him as thick as hail, so that, despite Christian's efforts, he was wounded in his head, hands, and feet, which made him give way a little. Apollyon took advantage of this circumstance and rushed at him with new vigor; but Christian, recovering himself, resisted as gallantly as he could.*
>
> *This furious combat lasted nearly half a day, until Christian's strength was nearly exhausted, because, due to his wounds, he was becoming weaker and weaker. Apollyon did not miss this advantage, and no longer with darts but hand to hand, he attacked him, with Christian dealing the last blow with his two-edged sword; then, after giving him a deadly thrust that made him give way, as one who has received the last blow. Seeing this, Christian recovered new vigor, attacked again, saying: "In all*

4. Freedman, Kaplan y Sadok. Tratado de Psiquiatría (Treaty of Psychiatry), Ed. Salvat, Barcelona, España, pág. 1381

these things we are more than conquerors through Him who loved us." Apollyon then opened his dragon wings and fled precipitously, and Christian did not see him again for a while.

During this combat, no one who has not seen and heard it, like me, can form an idea of how frightful and horrible were the shouts and roars of Apollyon, whose speech was like that of a dragon, and, on the other hand, how lamentable were the sighs and groans that Christian emitted, coming from his heart. Long was the fight and; nevertheless, not once did I see a pleasant look in his eyes, until he had wounded Apollyon with his two-edged sword; then yes, he looked up and smiled. Alas! This was the most terrible sight that I have ever seen.

After the fight, Christian thought of giving thanks to Him who had delivered him from the mouth of the lion, to Him who had helped him against Apollyon. And kneeling down, he said:

Beelzebub plotted my ruin,

Sending his messenger against me

To fight me with furious wrath,

And he would have defeated me in fierce struggle;

But helped me who dominates all,

And so I could drive him away with my sword.

To my Lord I owe the victory,

And I give Him thanks, praise, and glory.

John Bunyan was a faithful Christian who suffered from the mental illness we call obsessive compulsive disorder. He has been and continues to be a blessing even today through his writings, which are an inspiration to many Christians.

Dante Gebel (pastor, conference speaker, actor, producer, writer, singer, and radio and television host)

Dante Gebel was born on July 6, 1968, in the town of San Martín in Buenos Aires, Argentina, the youngest of the four children of Federico Gebel and Nelly Stokle. He studied as an electronic technician at the Werner von Siemens Technical School in Buenos Aires.

Gebel received Christ as his Savior in his childhood and began preaching at the age of 19. Today, Gebel is recognized in the Hispanic world as one of the most extraordinary speakers focused on youth and family, capable of leading the audience from laughter to tears with fascinating biblical storytelling. Currently, his messages are streamed worldwide, reaching an average of two million households each week, and he has four million followers on Facebook, one million on Instagram, and over one and a half million on his two YouTube channels.

From limitations to strength

Gebel experienced adverse conditions from birth. His father was an alcoholic, and his mother had suffered from cancer beginning in her pregnancy with Gebel. Gebel also has Asperger's syndrome, and in social contexts has endured mockery, criticism, and contempt. None of this would suggest the remarkable person he has become today. His limitations led him to develop the habits of reading, writing, and drawing, necessary skills for what was then his inability to speak in public.

At the age of 16, while working in a carpentry workshop, he had a serious accident, due to the clumsiness of movements, lack of agility, and poor motor skills characteristic of many people with Asperger's syndrome. Gebel he put his hand in a wood planer and had to have two fingers from his right hand reattached On April 24, 2014, Dante Gebel wrote on Facebook,

> *I am this child with sad, deep, and melancholic eyes. I have not been able to find a single photo of myself as a child laughing or even smiling; perhaps because my mother was dying of cancer since I was born and my father was an alcoholic, maybe because of my stuttering or my mild autism...or both. The teachers said that I was "introverted," "depressive," or as it was summed up in those times, "a very sad child."*
>
> *Both things. But one day, God decided that he would make me laugh for the rest of my life and that he would laugh with me...*
>
> *I had to deal with Asperger's syndrome that limited the way I related to other people; I couldn't understand double meanings or sarcasm, and people made fun of me; however, all of that did not prevent God from using me, and I am sure that it will not prevent him from using you either.*
>
> *Our potential does not depend on how good we are and what we can achieve by our own strength, but on a great God that we have, who is capable of overcoming our weaknesses to fulfill his purpose in our lives.*

On another occasion, he wrote,

> *The church should be the most authentic place on the planet. The church is for broken people, for people with problems, where one is transformed by the Lord; some remain in intensive care, in therapy, others change quickly... The Word says: we are growing according to the stature of the fullness of Christ."5*

Paul says in Philippians 1:12, *"Brothers, I want you to know that what has happened to me has really served to advance the gospel."* This is a truth in the life of Dante Gebel. God used his neurological disorder for the blessing of millions of people, many of them young, so that they could come to know Christ as their Savior. It is notable to see

5. Dante Gebel - La iglesia debería ser el lugar más auténtico (the church should be the most authentic place). diariolibre.com - https://bit.ly/3u6NxQ8

Pastor Gebel's concern for proclaiming the gospel to as many people as possible.

God has given Gebel an excellent memory, and he is intelligent and analytical, in addition to having a great facility for expressing ideas verbally. God uses his brilliant cognitive abilities, which enable him to deliver a clear, anointed, contextual, and powerful message every Sunday, reaching nearly a million people through different platforms and for over an hour, without the use of notes and without repeating the same content in a second service. In fact, in certain areas he exhibits special and superior skills to others.

Those who have this Asperger's are usually very responsible, noble, and loyal individuals. Dante Gebel has been loyal to the call of the Lord Jesus Christ to carry His name to the nations since his youth, and his specific superior abilities were placed in God's hands to accomplish a work that others in the same condition could not.

God can help develop the maximum potential in each of His faithful children who surrender their lives into His hands, regardless of any mental health struggles or illnesses. To repeat one of Gebel's phrases, "Someone has to say amen!!!"

Robert Schumann (musician and composer)

Born in 1818 in Germany, Schumann is considered one of the most important figures in musical romanticism. He composed four symphonies and wrote choral and religious music, chamber music, and music for piano.

This famous musical composer was inspired in his artistic production through severe emotional turbulence. Schumann experienced psychological ups and downs, alternately going through periods of intense creativity followed by depressive phases or moments. His marked emotional instability did not prevent him from becoming consecrated as one of the greatest musicians of all time. Could he have achieved so much if he had not suffered from these symptoms?

The emotional swings that we could describe today as bipolar disorder began in Schumann's youth. His illness was inherited from his mother, whom biographers describe as nervous and abnormally sensitive. Apparently, with the birth of Robert, she suffered an emotional disorder from which she never recovered. This also influenced his sister Emilia, who committed suicide when Schumann was 16 years old.

Schumann worked as a music critic, signing his articles in the newspaper Neue Zeitschrift with two pseudonyms: Florestan and Eusebius. He projected his conflicting extremes onto these personas: the impulsive, energetic, and cheerful Florestan strongly contrasted with the introverted, melancholic, and introspective Eusebius. At one point, when Schumann was going through a depressive period, he wrote: "Tuesday, all day and night, were the most horrible hours of my life. It was terrible. In the afternoon, a kind letter arrived from Clara [Schumann's wife] but it did not console me. Another moment, and I could not have endured that night. I couldn't close an eye. God save me from dying like this." This illustrates that Schumann considered the possibility of suicide.

One of Schumann's most prolific and productive moments occurred when he was going through a phase of psychic excitement. Over his entire career, he 246 lieder (a characteristic song of German romanticism, written for voice and piano, with lyrics as a lyric poem). He composed 136 of them in the short period of one year. "Since yesterday morning, I have written 27 pages of music, of which I can only say this: while I composed them, I laughed and cried with joy." He was going through a manic phase of his illness.

In a deep depressive state, Schumann left his house crying, intent on committing suicide in the Rhine River. After fishermen thwarted the attempt, he was interned in a clinic for the insane in Endenich. Schumann spent two years there before dying at the age of 46. At the time of his death, he was going through a depressive phase of his illness.

Artists and Bipolar Disorder

From ancient times to the present day, the phenomenon of bipolar disorder has caught the attention of mental health scholars as a unique alternation between mood states that dramatically sway a person between enthusiasm and discouragement.

This disorder is often seen in people who are involved in the world of art, probably because art is a suitable medium for expressing intense emotions and feelings. Whether it is due to the personalities of the artists or the nature of art itself, bipolar or manic-depressive disorder has been present with varying nuances and intensities among creators of all kinds throughout history.

In a way, people with artistic abilities experience a more intense lived experience than the average human being, and often exhibit sharp fluctuations between exalted and depressive states. Artists typically express a wide range of extreme experiences and sensations that they use to create their works, but as a counterpoint, they may sink into depression and even, in some cases, reach suicide.

There is a long list of artists, painters, writers, and musicians who have fallen victim to bipolar disorder, including Kurt Cobain, the singer, musician, and chief songwriter of the band Nirvana, one of the most influential rock musicians in the history of music. Cobain committed suicide by gunshot. Charles Baudelaire was a poet, essayist, and art critic, highly influential in French symbolism. Ernest Hemingway, a writer and journalist, was one of the foremost novelists and short story writers of the 20th century won the Pulitzer Prize for *The Old Man and the Sea* and the Nobel Prize in Literature for his complete works. Actress Vivien Leigh, a two-time Oscar winner for Best Actress and starred in *Gone with the Wind and A Streetcar Named Desire*, Tim Burton, film director, producer, and writer, is known for films such as *Batman* and *Charlie and the Chocolate Factory*. Leo Tolstoy is considered one of the most important writers in world literature, with his most famous works being *War and Peace and Anna Karenina.*

Notable figures of the Bible

King David

In his adolescence, David was a brave shepherd; in his youth he was a psalmist; and at the age of 30 he became the king of Israel. David was one of the most important kings in the history of Israel, unifying the territory of Judah and Israel. He was a brave warrior and a notable leader who reigned for seven years over Judah and 40 years over Israel. The Bible says that he was a man after God's own heart (Acts 13:22): "God removed [Saul] and replaced him with David, a man about whom God said, 'I have found David, son of Jesse, a man after my own heart; he will do everything I want him to do.'"

The distressing and stressful situations or periods David went through were many and prolonged. He was pursued by King Saul, who made several attempts on his life. Even as king, he felt deep guilt for sinning, his sons betrayed him, and some of them died or killed their brothers. Each experience reflects the hardship of his life and had a great impact on his emotions, as reflected in the psalms he wrote.

Expressing his depression, he wrote about his feelings in several psalms. In Psalm 32:3-4, he wrote, "*When I kept silent, my bones wasted away through my groaning all day long. For day and night your hand was heavy on me; my strength was sapped as in the heat of summer.*" He used the words "weak and miserable" to describe his loss of strength, lack of motivation, and apathy. "Groaning all day long" is a symptom of depression, and "my strength was sapped" reflects feeling dry inside, empty, and exhausted, another common symptom of depression.

In Psalm 38:4, David wrote, *"My guilt has overwhelmed me like a burden too heavy to bear."* Here, he mentions the burden of guilt weighing on his life (feelings of guilt are another common symptom of depression).

Then, in Psalm 38:6, we read: *"I am bowed down and brought very low; all day long I go about mourning."* And in Psalm 143:7m *"Answer me quickly, Lord; my spirit fails. Do not hide your face from me or I will be like those who go down to the pit."*

In the midst of his depressive state, David asked in Psalm 42:11, *"Why, my soul, are you downcast? Why so disturbed within me? Put your hope in God, for I will yet praise him, my Savior and my God."* In this verse, he questions his feelings of depression, decides not to remain in that situation, and turns to praise God. David's habit of speaking to himself and questioning his circumstances is positive, as the depressed person needs to talk to themselves instead of letting their feelings speak to and control their mind.

David did not lose his faith and trust in the Lord, and his prayers often came with expressions of pain and weeping. He asked many questions like: why do I feel guilty? Why do I isolate myself? Why do I feel rejected? What are my wrong attitudes? What do I need to change? Questions like these would have been valuable in helping David assess his mood. David understood this when he wrote Psalm 139:23-24, which says: *"Search me, God, and know my heart; test me and know my anxious thoughts. See if there is any offensive way in me, and lead me in the way everlasting."* Here, the psalmist, in a time of intimate reflection with the Lord his God, asks Him to confront his thoughts and seeks from God the understanding of why he feels the way he does.

David gives us clear evidence that a person who suffers from periods of depression can be a faithful believer because he has his faith in the living and true God. It also shows that even a person in a role of great importance (a king) may not have very good mental health and yet remain very useful in their sphere of influence.

The prophet Elijah

Elijah was an important prophet in the history of Israel who had a confrontation with the prophets of Baal. After a series of rituals and sacrifices, they could not prove the power of their god. When it was Elijah's turn, he proved to everyone that God is the only true God. Despite the success of this experience, once it was over, Queen Jezebel threatened Elijah with death and he had to flee. It was then that Elijah sank into deep anguish and depression. In that time, he felt so distressed and fearful that he asked God to take his life. This story is found in 1 Kings 18-19.

We see in this passage that after a situation of great bravery and determination, Elijah suffers emotional and physical exhaustion that leads him to be fearful and hesitant. Elijah knew both the power of God and the symptoms of depression.

If you are going through a depressive episode with dark thoughts and low self-esteem, you should know that the Bible tells us that Elijah was a person like us, who beyond having performed miracles and feats in the name of God was still someone who could get sick. The power of God also manifested itself on another occasion, despite Elijah's illness. As James 5:17 says, *"Elijah was a*

Elias experienced both the power of God and the symptoms of depression.

man with weaknesses like us, but he prayed fervently that it would not rain, and it did not rain on the earth for three and a half years." We can all learn to pray fervently like Elijah did. Still, we also see in Elijah's story that when he suffers from the depressive episode, he withdraws and isolates himself; he loses all his energy, becomes emotionally fatigued, feels sorry for himself, sleeps excessively, remains withdrawn, and only wants to be in bed. Totally discouraged, he distorts reality, believing that he is the only one in trouble, and becomes focused on the idea of death.

What a contrast between the desire to die—a product of his depressive symptom—and Elijah's true end on this earth when he is taken up by God to heaven without experiencing physical death! (2 Kings 2).

Naomi

Naomi was married to Elimelech and they lived in Bethlehem of Judah. Due to a famine, they moved to Moab with their husband and two sons. Within ten years, after her sons married wives Orpah and Ruth, Naomi's husband and two sons died without leaving any descendants. Naomi returned to Bethlehem with her daughter-in-law Ruth, who stayed with her. It has been proven that grief and immigration can cause depression, and losing a husband and two sons in a short period of time is a very difficult grief to overcome, especially in an unfamiliar environment. Naomi was no exception.

The name Naomi means sweet, and before all this loss, she probably was a sweet, cheerful, and optimistic woman.

When she returned to her homeland from Moab, the inhabitants barely recognized her. They asked, "Is this not Naomi?" They may have seen her as totally different, hunched over, wrinkled, with a furrowed brow, her face showing symptoms of depression; she had aged by more than just the passage of time. This was not something she could have hidden.

Naomi's soul was in such great grief that she asked those who recognized her not to call her Naomi anymore, but Mara, which means "bitter." Ruth 1:20 says, *"But she replied, 'Don't call me Naomi. Call me Mara, because the Almighty has made my life very bitter.'"* Her request reflects that her heart was filled with sadness and bitterness from the experiences she had gone through.

Depression also leads to a distortion of understanding of God, His care, and His purpose. Naomi says in Ruth 1:21, *"I went away full, but the Lord has brought me back empty. Why call me Naomi? The Lord has afflicted me; the Almighty has brought misfortune upon me."* Naomi saw God as someone who had turned His back on her and was responsible for sending calamity upon her. Feeling God distant and even blaming Him for losses or misfortunes is another symptom of severe depression. Still, Naomi is an example of a person who has faith in God can make good and appropriate decisions even while carrying a depressive episode when she decides to return to her homeland.

Naomi is an example of a depressed Christian who, despite her own pain, believes she can somehow bless others. This is what Naomi does with her daughter-in-law Ruth. For people going through a time of grief-induced depression, reaching out to others in love helps them overcome their pain.

Typically, a depressed person withdraws from social interaction, isolates themselves, does not think of others, and is absorbed in their own problems, but this was not Naomi's attitude. Instead, she opened up to Ruth and thought about how she could help and bless her. She advised and guided Ruth in a strategy to meet with their relative Boaz and to escape her vulnerability as a woman, foreigner, and widow. Helping Ruth was one of the ways through which Naomi resolved her depressive episode.

Job

Job was a very wealthy person with seven sons and three daughters, happily married and with many employees working for him. He is described as a God-fearing, blameless, and upright man; in other words, a faithful and true Christian. In Job 1:1 we read that *"In the land of Uz there lived a man named Job, a good man who feared God and shunned evil."* Can a person like this get sick and lose everything they have?

Going through illnesses or difficult situations is not shameful, and is not necessarily the result of a mistake or sin.

In some people's minds, leading a righteous life before God should preserve them from illnesses and calamities. When problems arise, some begin to doubt God's love and care and wonder why this is happening. The story of Job teaches us that the righteous can also suffer, and that in the face of illnesses, we must be patient and stand firm, as James 5:11 says: *"Indeed we count them blessed who endure. You have heard of the perseverance of Job and seen the end intended by the Lord—that the Lord is very compassionate and merciful."*

Job lost his children, his possessions, and his wealth, and also contracted an incurable disease. Some of his friends tried to encourage him, but later accused Job of hiding a sin that had caused all that harm. Still, Job never dared to deny or reject God. During his suffering, he asked many questions and reached a point where he wished he had not been born (wishing for death is a manifestation of depression). In Job 3:3-4 he says, *"May the day of my birth perish, and the night that said, 'A boy is conceived!' That day—may it turn to darkness; may God above not care about it; may no light shine on it."*

God allowed Job to go through extremely difficult and painful experiences, which ultimately led him to develop a much more intimate and real relationship with Him, as he expresses in Job 42:5: *"I had heard of you by the hearing of the ear, but now my eye sees you."* This is a vivid example of a Christian going through very difficult circumstances and remaining firm in faith.

Many, like Job, are going through very difficult situations and experiences of loss, illness, great distress, depression or anxiety, phobias, or low spirits, and many are fearful or feel defenseless. Are there answers for them?

Many of these answers can be found in Job. in him, we see a man who despite everything continued to trust in God, who is present even in mental health problems. Continuing to trust in Him, whether we understand it or not, is the key to moving forward. God can always be found in the midst of illness and can be seen as Job did, when he said, "I had heard of you by the hearing of the ear, but now my eye sees you."

Going through illnesses or difficult situations is not shameful, and is not necessarily the result of a mistake or sin. We find no guilt or sin in Job's life or in his family's life that would explain everything that happened to him. Illnesses can come, as well as economic or life losses, even in the best families. There are cases, like this one, where the purpose of suffering in the lives of His children is for the glory of God and the shame of Satan.

Prophet Jeremiah

Jeremiah was a Hebrew prophet, the son of a priest, who prophesied during the reigns of three kings (Josiah, Jehoiakim, and Zedekiah), delivering the message that they would be conquered by Babylon for turning away from God. He was a faithful and God-fearing man, destined to be a prophet from his mother's womb. His life had a clear mission. Jeremiah suffered pains and anguish for stubborn people who rejected the message that God had sent him to convey; he endured unjust and false defamation and slander, was imprisoned and sentenced to death, and often spoke in distress to the point of tears for rebellious people and those who were deaf to God's message. Far from being the weepy prophet—as some say of Jeremiah—he was a faithful, strong, and courageous man who, with perseverance and obedience, delivered the message God had given him, despite the circumstances he had to endure.

Jonah, the preacher

Jonah, a prophet during the reign of Jeroboam, receives God's indication to preach in Nineveh, the capital of Assyria, a very large city with about 120,000 inhabitants: *"The Lord sent this message to Jonah son of Amittai: 'Go to the great city of Nineveh and preach against it, because its wickedness has come up before me'"* (Jonah 1:1-2).

Johan was supposed to warn the inhabitants of Nineveh that the city would be destroyed in 40 days because of the sin within it, but he ignored that indication and got on a ship in the opposite direction of the city of Nineveh. Refusing to fulfill the will of God put him in a situation where he was on the verge of losing his life when he was swallowed by a great fish after being thrown into the sea from the ship he had taken to flee from God (this situation would generate severe stress for anyone).

Later, rescued by God, Jonah receives the indication again that he should go and preach to the inhabitants of Nineveh. God knew that Jonah was the one for this mission and that there was no one else with his personality traits. This time Jonah obeys, albeit reluctantly, and with great effort he preaches that the city will be destroyed by God in 40 days. Nineveh was an enemy city of the people of Israel and one that Jonah abhorred; the Assyrians were brutal, massacring their enemies, mutilating their captives, burning people alive, dismembering and beheading those they took prisoner.

Contrary to Jonah's expectations or personal desires, the results of his preaching were surprising: the entire city repented. Even the king, in a gesture of humility, ordered the entire city to fast to turn away God's wrath. It was an unprecedented situation: an entire city repented and God did not fulfill His warning. To achieve these results, Jonah must have exerted a great deal of effort. We know that he traveled through the villages for three days proclaiming that God was determined to destroy them if they did not repent of their wicked ways. Preaching and warning of God's punishment to a people Jonah did not love and achieving a result Jonah did not want (the salvation and mercy of God for an enemy people) angered Jonah greatly. It was difficult for Jonah to accept this calling. Jonah surely expected judgment and punishment from God for the Ninevites, but instead, he was the divine instrument for them to attain mercy.

We can postulate that Jonah was a person who had borderline personality disorder.

In a short time, Jonah went through a series of events that led him to say, in moments of anger and great frustration: "*Now, Lord, take away my life, for it is better for me to die than to live*" (Jonah 4:3). He was angry and wanted to die because of the great salvation God had granted to the city of Nineveh. Later, Jonah has the same feeling when God withers the plant that had grown to provide him shade from the scorching sun. In the face of searing heat, he once again becomes very angry, as we see in Jonah 4:9: "*Is it right for you to be angry about the plant?" God asked Jonah. "It is," he said. "And I'm so angry I wish I were dead.*" Jonah reacts this way because a plant that gave him shade withers away in the face of scorching sun; the magnitude of the response does not correlate with the reason for it.

We can postulate that Jonah was a person who had borderline personality disorder, but let's go through the symptoms to support this idea.

What are the symptoms of borderline personality disorder?

- Maintains intense and unstable relationships with others, leading to sudden changes from a close and loving relationship to rejection or extreme anger.
- Distorted and unstable self-image or sense of identity.
- Impulsive and often risky behavior.
- Self-destructive behavior, suicidal thoughts, or threatening to commit suicide.
- Intense and rapidly changing moods with episodes lasting from a few hours to several days; intense and inappropriate anger, or difficulty controlling anger.
- Difficulty trusting others, at times accompanied by irrational fear of other people's intentions.

We can identify many of these symptoms in Jonah's story: emotional outbursts, impulsive and risky behavior, even desiring death (he once told the sailors to throw him into the sea to certain death, and twice asked God to take his life). Jonah is a person of strong character and firm will, difficult to convince, courageous, outspoken, sincere; he does not hide his condition, as seen in Jonah 1:9-12: "'*I am a Hebrew, and I worship the Lord, the God of heaven, who made the sea and the land. This is my fault, for I am trying to run away from the presence of God,' he replied. The men were terrified and asked, 'Why did you do this? What should we do to you to make the sea calm down?' For the sea was getting rougher and rougher. 'Throw me into the sea,' he said to them, 'and the sea will calm down again. Because I know that this storm has come because of me.'*"

Through Jonah's actions, we see that he is determined, temperamental, and has an intimate knowledge of God, maintaining an intense and changing relationship with Him. He goes from recognizing His love and sovereignty to great anger for what He had done. While in the belly of the fish Jonah says, "*Those who trust in false gods do not know what they are missing; they despise the immense love of God. But I will forever pay you homage and offer ritual sacrifices in gratitude for what you have done for me. I will fulfill the promises I made to you. Only the Lord can save me!*" (Jonah 2:8-9).

In addition to this, Jonah was hot-tempered, determined, and firm; people like this are rarely willing to admit that any of their beliefs are wrong, and they find it difficult to be convinced of other viewpoints. God must break their will if they are to obey and fulfill their mission. In Jonah's case, this leads him to spend three days in the sea inside a large fish and fulfill the most extraordinary mission of his time; he is the person who brought the most people to repentance, conversion, and recognition of the living and true God. We see something similar in the New Testament with the Apostle Paul, who with fury, great determination, and much anger set off on the road to Damascus to exterminate Christians, but on the way was left blind for three days, during which God broke his will and transformed him into a servant as useful in His hands as no other of his time, bringing the gospel to the whole known world.

Can God use a person with such a strong character who gets so angry and can disobey Him? Yes, He can. On the other hand, how do you convert a population of 120,000 inhabitants through the message of a single person shouting in the street for three days? With the message of a man like Jonah.

Jonah 3:4 tells us that when he entered the city on the first day and began to preach, the people repented of their evil deeds. Jonah preached with a powerful voice the message of God, and the result was what we read in Jonah 3:5-9: "*The Ninevites believed the message*

God sent them and decided to fast. From the most exalted to the poorest, they dressed in mourning clothes, that is, in rough and coarse clothing, as a sign of repentance. When the king of Nineveh heard what Jonah was preaching, he came down from his throne, took off his royal robes, dressed in rough clothing, and sat on the ashes. Then the king and his nobles sent this message to the entire city: 'Let no one, including the animals, eat anything or drink water. Everyone must dress in rough mourning clothes, cry out to God with all their heart, and abandon their bad behavior, violence, and robbery. Perhaps God will have mercy, stop being angry with us, and allow us to continue living.'"

God uses a man with a difficult personality like Jonah because He understands his heart and the characteristics of his personality.

To achieve this result, Jonas probably preaches loudly and indignantly, telling them that everyone is going to die (something he intimately desired), so that the whole city understood through his passionate message the anger of God at their sins.

They understood God's fierce anger through the fierce anger with which Jonas preached to them, and it was most likely not a message of love or mercy. In fact, it was a message that generated a lot of fear.

God uses a man with a difficult personality like Jonas, insists on him, never tires of him, and gives him a second chance, because He understands his heart and the characteristics of his personality; perhaps this was the reason why God chose Jonah for such a mission.

Thank you, dear God, because you deign to use your faithful servants despite their problems, temperaments, and illnesses, and you treat them with your loving understanding and unconditional love.

Chapter 6

Guidelines to preserve and better mental health

In 3 John 2 we read, *"Dear friend, I pray that you may enjoy good health and that all may go well with you, even as your soul is getting along well."*

God wants us to be well and to have good health, not only in our bodies but in our entire being. As health professionals, we understand that the psychological and mental aspect of the human being is as important as everything else; if we are well with God, with ourselves, and with those around us, our work for the Lord will be more fruitful.

The care of our health is our responsibility at all stages of life.

The care of our health is our responsibility at every stage of life. Being healthy helps us to better exercise our gifts and abilities in all the roles we play and helps us to fulfill the call and mission we have, for the benefit of our quality of life, our service to God, and our relationships. In this chapter, we will describe some tips we can put into practice for better mental healthcare.

It's good to occasionally take a break in the journey of life and review how we are doing. The assessment you will see next is a list of 28 statements. If you identify with 15 or more of them, you are probably under pressure and should consider some changes in your lifestyle to prevent the possibility of getting sick. Later on, you will find some tips to improve your score and your health.

Emotional health assessment

Carefully read each sentence and mark those that you identify as true for you.

- I receive more than 25 messages per day
- I find it difficult to relax and do nothing
- I get nervous or irritated when I have to wait
- I can't stay still; I always move some part of my body
- Lately I feel more tired than usual
- I have had frequent episodes of anxiety
- I have trouble sleeping
- I feel tired when I wake up
- I have headaches and muscle tension
- My acquaintances tell me to slow down a bit
- I cut people off when they're talking or tune out of what they are saying
- I have palpitations, dizziness, and dizziness
- I have frequent urination (may be an indicator of anxiety)
- I feel emotionally drained during church services
- I treat some people as if they are impersonal objects
- Dealing with people all day is an effort for me

- I have become more insensitive to other people
- I feel frustrated in church services
- My body weight has varied recently
- I think I am working too hard
- Ministering to others causes me stress
- I feel that that others blame me for some of their problems
- It makes me angry when other people don't change
- I feel guilty for the lack of growth in the people in my life
- Being loved is important to me
- I perform tasks faster and more efficiently than others
- It annoys me to see things being done that I could do more quickly and efficiently
- I have difficulty separating personal life from family life.

1. Attending to your own health

Health is dynamic and fluctuating, and can change throughout life. Every pastor or church leader is vulnerable to illness, as are their families and congregation members. We should be concerned about health, especially if we are involved in the care and ministry of others, some of whom may be mentally ill.

There are many aspects we should take into account. For example, what were the past experiences of illness and loss, both in our immediate family and in previous generations? Can you remember how other members of the family responded to them?

We have all been through suffering, illness, or loss, but not everyone responds in the same way. Illnesses vary; stories and family systems are different from person to person, and each one of us has a unique personality.

Ask yourself how you were cared for as a child when you were not feeling well or needed help. It is common for adults to provide the same type of care that we received in childhood. Positive experiences of healing and care can be excellent resources in encounters with others who are ill. If the experiences in childhood were negative, we may feel resentment, feelings of guilt, or shame around them.

Ask yourself: in your life or in your family history do you notice any unmet needs or unresolved illnesses? This may be something you feel uncomfortable talking about. Our own unresolved experiences and needs can make it difficult to approach others who are suffering and going through similar issues.

You must know your own limits. This is key to effective pastoral care. You cannot do it all. In fact, thinking you can is arrogant. Adequate self-care is essential. In order to care for others, you must first care for yourself. Most of us have heard the example from flight attendants on airplanes: in case of depressurization, capable adults should first put on their own oxygen masks, then help children and the elderly around you. If you do not put on your own oxygen mask on time, in just 15 seconds you can experience symptoms such as fatigue, headache, tiredness, confusion, and coordination problems, and you will not be able to help those around you. Aren't these symptoms similar to emotional fatigue in the face of the demands of ministry without a balance with healthcare?

Many people feel more comfortable giving care than receiving it. Some deny their own conflicts because the role they play is that of a helper and they never admit that they need help. If you, as a pastor or minister, are seen by your congregation as a strong pillar who is immune to grief and suffering, who never feels pain and can always help everyone, you could be in trouble.

We tend to set very high standards for ourselves, thinking that if we have a calling from God everything will be fine and there will never be any problems. This only adds to the impression that pastors have it all together. People may wonder, "How could the pastor be stressed or depressed, or suffer from an anxiety disorder?" The pastor may think of their own struggles, "Let no one find out," or, if they do choose to share with someone, "Let it stay between us." If faith leaders avoid turning to mental health professionals with their struggles, a possible clinical condition could worsen. It's also important to remember the example this sets for the congregation. If faith leaders always present themselves as strong and immune to problems because of their intimate relationship with God, a member of the congregation who has mental health problems may question whether they really have the same God as the pastor, leading to frustration and doubt.

It is necessary to rethink what your illusions and expectations were when entering the ministry. Are your expectations being fulfilled? If they are not, how does that affect your mood and well-being? God's minister carries many human burdens on their shoulders, has many meetings to participate in, many messages to respond to, many people to follow up with. People want you to listen to them and talk to them, and they want your advice, your knowledge, and your blessing. People are often unaware of pastors' schedules and the amount of time you are dedicating to these types of conversations and duties. These tasks generate a high psychological demand over which you have little control and autonomy: unexpected calls, requests for help, schedules interrupted by emergencies, and unexpected events, meetings that extend beyond what was planned, generating an excess of hours invested. This constant demand can lead to fatigue and exhaustion. Pastors are always with people, which is why when you arrive home you may not feel like playing or interacting with your children or talking to your wife or husband; you may only desire to be in silence. This entire situation is not healthy, and if you or someone in your family is going through an emotional problem, how do you face it?

You may feel unprepared for every decision you have to make, or to absorb all the conflicts of the congregation like a sponge. This inability only generates more stress. During the COVID-19 pandemic, many pastors and leaders made an effort to help members of the congregation and the community who were going through difficult situations: they cooked, delivered groceries, reached out to those who were having a hard time, and offered prayer and counseling. This effort resulted in pastors and leaders experiencing the deterioration of their health, physical exhaustion and fatigue, sleep disturbances, and distress. Their fears increased, as did their perception of the risk of contagion and the impact that COVID-19 could have on their personal life and family. Data from a statistical study shows that those who sacrificed individual goals for the common good due to their empathy and their social assistance activities exaggerated the risk of contagion and negative impacts of COVID-19.[1]

Accepting your own limitations, setting boundaries with those who invade your space, and asking for help or delegating tasks is a sign of strength and wisdom.

Accepting one's own limitations, setting boundaries with those who disrupt due to their own needs, and asking for help or delegating is a sign of strength and wisdom. Being human is accepting vulnerability; we should not feel ashamed of needing help.

Financial concerns are also significant for pastors and faith leaders. Worry over your family's financial needs, medical coverage, whether you'll earn a monthly income that covers your daily expenses without getting into debt, and whether you'll save enough to someday retire

1. The price of prosociality in pandemic times. Socialscience.nature.com - https://go.nature.com/3np1xkn

are all burdens. Life is more peaceful when those financial concerns are not issues, but for pastors, that is rarely the case.

One very negative type of relationship that has increased during the long period of the pandemic and lockdown is codependency. This can occur between pastors or faith leaders and members of the congregation. Codependency arises when we show an excessive and inappropriate concern for another person's difficulties, resulting in the loss of interpersonal boundaries. Typically, this is a relationship between demanding people who become dependent on you, and you in turn start to overprotect them, telling them as often as daily what they should or shouldn't do to feel better. You feel responsible for their problems or feelings, upset when you see no changes, angry when they don't follow your advice, guilty for the lack of progress in their spiritual lives, or depressed and frustrated if they move away from you or join another congregation. By taking care of them, you stop taking care of yourself and your family, even sacrificing family time. They call you at any time and you spend hours trying to advise them on their problems. Codependent relationships are an emotional drain that can exhaust you or make you sick.

If you are experiencing a situation like this, acknowledge the problem, find a way to remove yourself from excessive involvement, identify if you have feelings of anger or guilt, relearn how to help, and establish clear boundaries. Send a clear message to the congregation that you are a regular person with struggles and difficulties, someone who prays for others and also needs others to pray for you. Pastors are not the only ones who can support congregation members. It's likely that there is a percentage of mature congregation members who have experienced emotional problems and have successfully resolved them, and are now able to provide help to others. 1 Corinthians 12:25-27 says, "*...each one should care for the others. If one member suffers, all the members suffer with him; and if one member receives honor, all the others rejoice with him. You are all part of the body of Christ, and each one is a necessary member of that body.*"

2. Awareness and mental health

Our conscience is a mental function. Our conscience points out or reproaches us if we have done something that is not good or that is displeasing to God. It is not a spiritual gift or something supernatural or divine, but rather part of our mental capacity given by God to be able to detect our mistakes and sins and seek the solution in repentance, confession, and change. Our conscience evaluates, like a gauge, if something is wrong. We have the free will to make decisions based on the guiding of our conscience.

a. A good conscience is necessary to be a good witness, to love fully, and to not become shipwrecked in the faith. We read in Acts 24:16, *"So I strive always to keep my conscience clear before God and man."* Paul gives great importance to having a clear conscience. Feeling guilty for having done something that is wrong is correct and commendable, but feeling guilt due to excessive demands could lead to emotional disturbances. The conscience has been altered by the presence of sin in the world since the Fall in Eden, and it can falsely detect guilt: this is what we call in psychology false guilt. Servants of God may feel this type of guilt for actions that have not been carried out or for which they are not responsible.

The conscience can lose its function if it is not listened to or if it is shut off.

Do you feel guilty for an act or situation that has not been corrected and for which you are not responsible? Or for something you have not been able to do? Do you feel guilty for not having obtained something you believe you should have achieved? Do you feel guilty for not having done something you could not do? Is there a sin from the past that has already been forgiven and still hurts you today? Do you self-punish by speaking ill of yourself or feeling of little worth? Some of these situations could be altering your emotions and damaging your mental health.

b. On the other hand, the conscience may be pointing out that something needs to be changed. David's story shows us how damaging it is to not listen to the conscience, and that the relief and mental and spiritual healing that come when we pay attention to it will rectify our lives: *"Blessed is the one whose transgressions are forgiven, whose sins are covered. Blessed is the one whose sin the Lord does not count against them and in whose spirit is no deceit. When I kept silent, my bones wasted away through my groaning all day long. For day and night your hand was heavy on me; my strength was sapped as in the heat of summer"* (Psalms 32:1-4).

The conscience can lose its function if it is not listened to or if it is shut off. When this occurs, we lose the ability to discern whether a behavior is right or if the feelings we are experiencing are the result of having done something wrong. It is possible to continue sinning without feeling anything because the conscience loses its edge.

It is possible to continue sinning without feeling anything because the conscience loses its edge.

c. As Christians, we are responsible for atoning for offenses toward God or others. We must identify those actions, ask for forgiveness, and, if possible, make restitution if we have caused harm. 1 Peter 3:16 says, *"keeping a clear conscience, so that those who speak maliciously against your good behavior in Christ may be ashamed of their slander."* The apostle Peter is telling us that a clear conscience is fundamental to our testimony.

The apostle Paul also tells us in 1 Timothy 1:5, *"The goal of this command is love, which comes from a pure heart and a good conscience and a sincere faith."* The ability to love fully is related to a clear conscience and sincere faith. What a good combination!

In 1 Timothy 1:18-19 we read, *"Timothy, my son, I am giving you this command in keeping with the prophecies once made about you, so that by recalling them you may fight the battle well, holding on to faith and a good conscience, which some have rejected and so have suffered shipwreck with regard to the faith."* In these passages, we see that a clear conscience is closely related to faith.

d. In addition, a conscience purified by the sacrifice of Christ on the cross of Calvary will help us to serve the Lord in a better way, as the author of Hebrews tells us: *"For by one sacrifice he has made perfect forever those who are being made holy"* (Hebrews 10:14).

e. In medicine, altered states of consciousness are discussed, which can lead to severe mental deterioration. Drawing a parallel with what we are mentioning, we see the importance of consciousness in maintaining good health.

Altered states of consciousness include:

- Decreased alertness: the person is unaware of the danger they are in and does not pay attention to warning signs. They tend to be less aware of what is happening around them and think more slowly than usual. They may appear tired.
- Mental confusion: the person is unsure of the decisions they need to make, and unable to find the best course of action to take. They are unable to think as clearly and quickly as they usually do. They may feel disoriented and have difficulty paying attention, remembering, and making decisions.
- Stupor: the person is consistently drowsy, dull, and unresponsive to the needs around them. Stupor resembles a typical depressive state.

Check your consciousness periodically to maintain good mental health.

3. Lifestyle and mental health

Lifestyle includes eating, physical activity, rest, the management of resources (time, effort, and money), alcohol or tobacco consumption, and also includes habits, behaviors, and actions, education, what is read, types of entertainment and pastimes, relationships, and which media are consumed. All of these factors may, to some extent, impact health or illness.

One can better bless others when they lead a healthy lifestyle.

You can check how you're doing with your own lifestyle by going back to the beginning of this chapter and examining the questions found there. You should check if you are living according to the prevailing culture and trends of the time, or with principles that contribute to maintaining overall health, reducing risk factors that may affect it.

Many mental health illnesses have disordered sleeping as a main symptom, and most mental illnesses worsen if you do not sleep well

It is said that there are five points to consider for a good lifestyle: eat half, chew twice, walk three times, laugh four times, and pray without ceasing.

4. Sleeping well and mental health

Good rest and sleeping well are important for health. Many mental illnesses have disordered sleeping as a main symptom, and most mental illnesses worsen if you do not sleep well. Many disorders arise after being subjected for a long time to work or academic demands, or to negative experiences that generate worries and thoughts that swirl in the mind like a blender. This generates an excessive consumption of neurotransmitters that, if you are not sleeping well, cannot be replenished; that is why good rest is so important.

The body dedicates about a third of life to sleep. Sleep is a physiological need as essential as food and hydration, and necessary to maintaining good health. According to Psalm 127:2, "*In vain you rise early and stay up late, toiling for food to eat—for he grants sleep to those he loves.*" We must see sleep as an ally to health. Sleeping through the night is an invaluable exercise in physical and mental restoration. During sleep, hunger hormones are balanced, muscles and bones are repaired and grow, and the body's defenses are strengthened. Sleep aids in learning and memory.

The recommended amount of sleep according is ten to thirteen hours for kids ages 3 to 5, nine to eleven hours for kids age 6-13, eight to ten hours for teens age 14-17, and seven hours or more for adults.

Some tips to get good sleep:

- Do not go to bed too full or hungry. It is ideal to have dinner at least two hours before going to bed, allowing enough time for digestion so it does not interfere with sleep. Going to bed hungry can be counterproductive because it can disrupt sleep throughout the night.
- Exercising at least three hours before bedtime can facilitate sleep, and exercising immediately before going to bed is not recommended. When the body temperature begins to decrease, the tendency to sleep increases. Body temperature rises during exercise and may remain elevated for few hours, which can interfere with sleep.
- Having a routine and relaxing activity before bedtime will facilitate better sleep. Taking a warm bath (the body temperature increases during a bath, but decreases rapidly

afterward), reading, or listening to music can also help, as well as reading the Bible and listening to songs of praise to God.

- Most people sleep better in a cool, quiet, and dark environment. It is good to eliminate noise and other distractions, and avoid an environment that is too humid, dry, warm, or cold. The bedding, mattress, and pillow should be comfortable.
- Avoid eating, watching television, using the phone, or using any type of device in bed to avoid neuronal stimulation.
- If you wake up during the night and do not fall back asleep within 30 minutes, get up, drink warm milk, get some fresh air, take a short walk, read something, pray, and do not go back to bed until you feel sleepy.
- Avoid looking at the phone during the night to check the time or see how much time is left until morning This usually causes anxiety. Avoid looking at phones or computers until it's time to get up.
- If you are very tired, take a nap during the day as needed, but keep it to 30-40 minutes (any longer and you may wake up feeling groggy).
- Avoid caffeine before bedtime; caffeine is a stimulant and can interfere with sleep. Caffeine from products such as coffee, tea, soda, and chocolate remains in the body for an average of three to five hours, but can affect some people for up to 12 hours. Avoiding caffeine six hours before bedtime can help improve sleep.
- Try to go to bed and wake up at the same time every day. Avoid sleeping in more on weekends to prevent sleep problems during the week, and can generate fatigue or headaches.

5. Light, movement, and mental health.

Confinement, lack of sensory stimulation and lack of exercise are enemies of mental health.

Light

- Generally, those who have mental illness seek to be inside the house, often with the windows closed. If you are supporting someone with mental illness, it can be beneficial if you encourage them to open the windows, go for a walk on a nice day, and do some exercise or gymnastics, or simply sit in the sun. Sunlight is beneficial as it promotes the production of neurotransmitters related to pleasure. Sunlight helps us to relax, rest more fully, and contributes to an improved mood. The longer the period of light exposure, the greater a person's overall sense of well-being, the more energy they have, and the more active and creative they are.
- Sunbathing decreases depressive symptoms. Many of us recognize the lack of energy and motivation we feel when facing a gray and cloudy day. Sunlight influences the production of melatonin. This leads to a healthy cycle where sleep comes naturally when it is dark outside, and we awake in the morning when it's light.
- Sunlight also influences the brain's neurotransmission systems. Light stimulates the hypothalamus, which impacts many functional aspects such as sleep, feeding, and body temperature control. These functions are ones that are dysregulated due to mental disorders.
- Light also influences the synthesis of serotonin, an important neurotransmitter involved in maintaining a good mood. Outdoor exposure on a sunny day offers 300 times more light than remaining inside in artificial lighting. It's important for people to have access to bright light for the longest possible

time. The recommended hours for sunbathing are in the morning until 11 a.m. (at the latest), and in the afternoon, from 4 p.m. on.

Movement

- It's common for those with mental illness to remain immobile for long periods, often in bed or slumped in a chair. After spending long periods without moving, people feel sluggish. Movement plays an important role in improving depression and other disorders.
- Blood is oxygenated better. Exercise helps to clean the blood, clearing the arteries of toxins.
- With exercise, endorphins are also produced. Endorphins are known as the hormone of well-being, and they generate feelings of wellness, relaxation, and satisfaction, increasing concentration and self-esteem, making the sick person feel better, and decreasing anxiety and tension.
- It is difficult to establish a routine of regular exercise. Exercise may not feel fun and it can be intimidating to make yourself exercise if you don't want to. Afterward, though, the person will find that they feel much better. The choice of type of exercise is a matter of physical constitution, age, and pre-existing health. An exercise that is accessible to everyone, is free and simple, can be done in all seasons of the year, and is available for all ages, is walking. Walking for half an hour several days of the week offers many advantages and can be just as beneficial as more demanding activities.
- People who have a hard time exercising consistently often benefit from having an exercise partner, which gives an incentive to keep going and maintain consistency. It is important that this other person is someone whose age or needs are similar to theirs so that they are able to do work out at a

similar intensity. In the beginning, people should not begin with strenuous exercise or long durations. It is better to work out consistently for shorter periods and/or lower intensity than with more intensity but no consistency.

- Taking a short walk at some point in the day, especially in the sun, is a good habit. Although it may be difficult, starting to walk is a way for a person with mental illness to remind themselves that they can still function despite the illness.

6. Time management and mental health

We read in Ecclesiastes 3:1-8,

> *For everything there is a season, and a time for every matter under heaven: a time to be born, and a time to die; a time to plant, and a time to pluck up what is planted; a time to kill, and a time to heal; a time to break down, and a time to build up; a time to weep, and a time to laugh; a time to mourn, and a time to dance; a time to throw away stones, and a time to gather stones together; a time to embrace, and a time to refrain from embracing; a time to seek, and a time to lose; a time to keep, and a time to throw away; a time to tear, and a time to sew; a time to keep silence, and a time to speak; a time to love, and a time to hate; a time for war, and a time for peace. What gain has the worker got from his toil?*

Many emotional problems are caused or exacerbated by poor time management. Some people always procrastinate their tasks, others are always rushing to finish what they need to do. They have breakfast or lunch standing up because they don't have time, they don't chew and digest properly. Others live anxiously waiting for things to happen, and are restless waiting for a train or a bus, sometimes even waiting for a traffic light to turn green. Others worry about not being able to complete their commitments on a day filled with responsibilities. All of this generates a high level of stress that affects emotions.

Managing time means controlling it efficiently. It is a myth to think that in the future you will have more time. If you do not manage your time now, when your day has 24 hours, you will not do it in the future when your day also has 24 hours.

It is a myth to think that in the future you will have more time. If you don't manage your time now, when your day has 24 hours, you won't do it in the future when your day also has 24 hours.

Frequent situations that lead to difficult time management include unnecessary meetings, interruptions, mental fatigue due to lack of good rest, unclear priorities, indecision, communication failures, delegation failures, personal disorganization, waiting for a response that does not come, and too-prolonged time spent on hobbies.

Some questions to reflect on: Do you control your time or do others do it for you? Does your life have free time—time to think, time alone, time for family, time to share, time to pray? When the alarm clock goes off in the morning, do you have to jump out of bed running because otherwise you will be late for work? Or do you get up calmly and have time to eat breakfast, pray to entrust the day to the Lord, and greet all the members of your family?

Time can be described as a succession of events. If your work starts at 8 a.m. and at 8 a.m. you are still at home, with a half-hour commute to work, you will probably start your day very poorly. If instead you organize activities according to the time each one demands, you will not be rushing and running out of time. A common phrase of those who do not manage time well is, "I'm very sorry, but I didn't have time to make it to your birthday." What they are really saying is,

"At the time of your birthday, I was elsewhere doing something else." You cannot be in two places at the same time.

Ephesians 5:15-16 advises us, "*Be very careful, then, how you live—not as unwise but as wise, making the most of every opportunity...*" Time derives from the word "cronos," which is a period, a measure of time. With "cronos" we measure time in hours, days, years; from "cronos" comes the word "chronometer," which is an instrument for measuring time intervals.

Genesis 1:14-18 says,

> *And God said, "Let there be lights in the vault of the sky to separate the day from the night, and let them serve as signs to mark sacred times, and days and years." And it happened. So God made the two great lights: the greater light to govern the day and the lesser light to govern the night. He also made the stars. God set them in the vault of the sky to give light on the earth, to govern the day and the night, and to separate light from darkness. And God saw that it was good.*

To measure earthly times, God established the creation of the sun, the moon, and the stars. That is why the units of measurement of our time are the millennium, century, year, month, day, hours, etc. It is the time of man that we can measure.

7. Weekly rest and mental health

There is an important reality: Our energy is a limited resource. No one has an infinite capacity for emotional and physical energy. Working without rest causes overwhelm, and when reserves are depleted, problems can arise.

In Genesis 2:1-3 we read, "*Thus the heavens and the earth were completed in all their vast array. By the seventh day God had finished the work he had been doing; so on the seventh day he rested from all his work. Then God blessed the seventh day and made it holy, because on it he rested from all the work of creating that he had done."* This passage tells us that God deliberately stopped working and rested. He rested for a whole day, and blessed that day (something He did not do with the other days). By His example, God wants to teach us several important things that help us maintain good mental health. In Isaiah 58:13 it says: "If you keep your feet from breaking the Sabbath and from doing as you please on my holy day, if you call the Sabbath a delight and the Lord's holy day honorable, and if you honor it by not going your own way and not doing as you please or speaking idle words."

a) God wants to teach us the principle of resting one day per week. The day of rest is called shabbat (Sabbath), which means "to stop doing, rest, refresh, stop running, rest." In Exodus 23:12 we read, *"Six days do your work, but on the seventh day do not work..."*. In these passages we find God's advice to maintain a day of weekly rest.

b) Another teaching for this Sabbath day, beyond rest, is liberation. This is a day for freeing oneself from the worries of the week, the burdens and anxiety, and being able to relax, to stop thinking only about work. There is a very close relationship between Sabbath and the liberation of the people of Israel from the slavery of Egypt.

Deuteronomy 5:12-15 tells us: *"Observe the Sabbath day by keeping it holy, as the Lord your God has commanded you. Six days you shall labor and do all your work, but the seventh day is a Sabbath to the Lord your God... Remember that you were slaves in Egypt and that the Lord your God brought you out of there with a mighty hand and an outstretched arm. Therefore the Lord your God has commanded you to observe the Sabbath day."*

c) Another teaching is to honor God on this day. In Isaiah 58:13 it says: *"If you keep your feet from breaking the Sabbath and from doing as you please on my holy day, if you call the Sabbath a delight and the*

Lord's holy day honorable, and if you honor it by not going your own way and not doing as you please or speaking idle words." Here we understand another teaching: This passage tells us that the day of rest is a gift, it is a delight, and it is glorious. Taking a break is a commandment, a gift, and a task, the task of honoring God.

So, what purpose does God have in mind for this weekly rest? It is a break from stress, from wear and tear. It is time for resting in the Lord, in His arms, having intimacy with Him. It is time for gathering in family, meditating and praying together, reading the Bible and sharing. The Sabbath gives time to reflect, seek God's guidance and direction for decisions, recover from the wounds of the week, and for spiritual enrichment; this is God's will. Facing problems will be much more effective and we will not be so exhausted if we follow this advice to take a weekly day of rest. We must stop working, as Luther says, so that God can work in us.

For the person with mental illness, the evidence of bad humor is often heightened. Bad humor generates despair, insecurity, restlessness, helplessness, pessimism, and apathy: the complainer always sees everything as bad.

There will always be unexpected things that crop up to demand of our time. If we have no margin, when disruptions occur it will only feel more stressful and subtract even more from rest. We need to practice saying "Not this time" to some invitations. We need to think about what tasks we can leave for another tome or delegate to someone else. All of this will lead to better weekly rest.

8. Good humor and mental health

"Humor" in this case refers to a person's disposition at any given time. Being in "good humor" means a person can respond to life's various situations in a cheerful, optimistic way; this attitude helps make difficult moments in life more bearable. When someone is in "bad humor," they will respond to what life brings with complaints, anger, and irritability.

For the person with mental illness, the evidence of bad humor is often heightened. Bad humor generates despair, insecurity, restlessness, helplessness, pessimism, and apathy; the complainer always sees everything as bad. On the other hand, good humor generates a positive attitude toward life and generates health. A positive attitude is learned; laughing and good humor are, too.

A positive attitude is learned: laughing and good humor too.

Related to "good humor" is a "good sense of humor." Some people have a good sense of humor, meaning the ability to make others laugh or entertain others or themselves through a variety of situations. A good sense of humor creates a confident atmosphere, increases energy, prevents stress, improves facial expression, reduces tension, and increases the desire to live. A good sense of humor generates a feeling of subjective well-being, strengthens the immune system, de-dramatizes adverse situations, and reduces stress, anxiety, and depression; releases endorphins and adrenaline, reduces cortisol levels, helps reduce fears, releases tension and insecurity, improves planning and problem solving, and reduces negative thoughts.

Having a good sense of humor does not mean that one is not serious or is superficial. Maintaining good humor, and a good sense of humor, is a real challenge in current times.

"A joyful heart is good medicine, but a broken spirit dries up the bones" (Proverbs 17:22). This text tells us that having a good sense of humor prolongs our lives and is an economical and effective medicine. Proverbs 15:15 says, *"For the despondent, every day brings trouble; for the happy heart, life is a continual feast."* Psalm 5:11 says, *"But let all who take refuge in you be glad; let them ever sing for joy. Spread your protection over them, that those who love your name may rejoice in you."* In Philippians 4:4 we read, *"Rejoice in the Lord always. I will say it again: Rejoice!"* And in 1 Thessalonians 5:16-18 it says, *"Be joyful always ... for this is God's will for you in Christ Jesus."*

9. Thoughts and mental health

Many illnesses have symptoms of negative, sick, obsessive, delusional, bitter, or distorted ideas. Ideas generate thoughts that then influence behavior. What ideas do you keep in your mind? Ideas arise from what is read, heard, and seen; the things that interest us are what hold our attention. The ideas and thoughts we generate go on to shape our lives.

The most vulnerable when it comes to thoughts and ideas are children: their mental map is still forming, and as they receive news and information, they have no previous experiences to compare it to, no previous data to use to interpret what they read, hear, or see.

Many children and young people spend many hours in front of screens (adults too!): TV, internet, movies, games, videos, and social platforms can impact children's minds with displays of crime, extreme violence, anti-biblical values, immorality, hatred, revenge, and even pornography. Children's ideas, thoughts, and behaviors will be influenced by all that they see.

The filters for interpreting the content we see or hear are found in the Word of God and in the discernment given to us by the Holy Spirit. In Romans 12:2 we read, *"Do not conform to the pattern of this world, but be transformed by the renewing of your mind. Then you will be able to test and approve what God's will is—his good, pleasing and perfect will."* The Bible says that we can change our way of thinking. This is why God made our brains moldable, capable of being modified according to how we use and stimulate them, and according to the things we pay attention to. Let's think frequently about the blessings and promises God has given us, and stimulate our minds by praying, reading the Bible, and remembering all the blessings we have received from the Lord. This will bring peace to our lives and emotions.

We find biblical advice in Philippians 4:8: *"Finally, brothers and sisters, whatever is true, whatever is noble, whatever is right, whatever is pure, whatever is lovely, whatever is admirable—if anything is excellent or praiseworthy—think about such things."* And in Proverbs 4:20-22 we read, *"My son, pay attention to what I say; turn your ear to my words. Do not let them out of your sight, keep them within your heart; for they are life to those who find them and health to one's whole body."*

You can decide which memory album to open. We must be wise in managing our memories and discard those that harm us.

The Bible says we can choose to discard the thoughts that are not beneficial. What you think about impacts the vision you have of life. Think about how to nurture your mind. Thoughts can generate health or illness. Our minds can help us to confront reality, to understand what we are experiencing, and to make wise decisions.

Let us use this capability that God has given us for a better quality of life.

10. Memories and forgetfulness that generate mental health

Thinking is also remembering. Memory has substance. The brain contains numerous albums of memories, some beautiful, others sad, and others distressing. Life experiences are archived in our memory—and our memory is something that can be trained. Each of us can decide which memory album to open. We must be wise in managing our memories and in discarding those that harm us.

It is necessary to manage these memories in a healthy way. There are memories that appear in the focus of our consciousness and that we should forget; that is, we should set them aside, not pay attention to them, and eventually discard them.

a) One type that should be discarded is bitter memories. Hebrews 12:15 tells us, *"See to it that no one falls short of the grace of God and that no bitter root grows up to cause trouble and defile many."* Painful and distressing memories must be cast out of the mind, for they poison our own lives and the lives of those around us: they may have to do with comparing ourselves to others, making us feel inferior; they may arise from resentment over something that is difficult to forgive; perhaps we still feel guilty about something that God has already pardoned.

b) Personal relationships from the past that have generated sadness or bitterness and still have influence should also be forgotten. As an example, in 1 Samuel 16:1 we read, *"The Lord said to Samuel, 'How long will you mourn for Saul, since I have rejected him as king over Israel? Fill your horn with oil and be on your way; I am sending you to Jesse of Bethlehem. I have chosen one of his sons to be king.'"* God's advice to Samuel was to forget the loss of a relationship that caused him grief. Are there members of the congregation who left without even saying goodbye, after having worked with them for years? Are you still mourning over that loss? If we are angry or hurt by abandonment or the loss of a relationship, God's advice is to look ahead, because there are many others who still need to be blessed. In Isaiah 43:18 it says, *"Forget the former things; do not dwell on the past."*

In Exodus 17:14 it says, *"Then the Lord said to Moses, 'Write this on a scroll as something to be remembered...'"* The Bible is full of meaningful stories and good reminders, so it's a good habit to read it every day. Reading the Bible helps maintain a healthy mind.

If you frequently read the Bible, its promises and advice can be a good album to bring to mind often, especially in times when you have to make decisions or in moments of worry and uncertainty. A beautiful example of bringing good memories from the Bible to mind is that of Mary, the mother of Jesus. When the angel announced to her that she was going to have a child, she—at the time a young teenager—lifted a beautiful song of praise to God full of quotes from the Old Testament (Luke 1:46-55). Mary recalled passages she had already treasured in her memory and heart. What sensitivity her parents had to transmit the Word of God to their children, and what wisdom Mary had to treasure them in her heart!

In the face of important events, decisions that need to be made, situations to understand or accept, we can be like Mary and recall biblical passages that offer guidance and advice. Even as we go through struggles, suffering, and illness, let us remember that God loves us and keeps His promises. In Hebrews 10:32 it says, *"Remember those earlier days after you had received the light, when you endured in a great conflict full of suffering."* These words remind us of a principle that we should always keep in mind: Accepting Christ as Savior and receiving the light of the Gospel does not guarantee the absence of struggle, suffering, and illness. Let us always remember it.

II. Social links and mental health

Our contemporary society is characterized by loneliness and isolation; even in our churches, no matter how many people attend them, some members feel lonely or struggle to maintain masks of success and well-being that distance them from others. People will mask their shortcomings, guilt, or needs, keeping distance from others, but soon they suffer from loneliness even when in a large group of known people whom they call "friends."

The development and functioning of the brain are influenced by interaction with others. Who we spend time with impacts how we see ourselves, think, and function. Other people can influence us in a health or unhealthy way.

Sharing our personal concerns, experiences, or worries with trusted others makes us more aware and gives us a clearer and better understanding of reality. The Bible says in Proverbs 27:17, "*As iron sharpens iron, so one person sharpens another.*" The NLT version says, "*As iron sharpens iron, so a friend sharpens a friend.*"

By sharing our experiencing and thoughts with a friend, we also come to know our own strengths and weaknesses. With a friend, we can share burdens and needs, cry with them if necessary, and learn to check and trust our emotions. When we share with wise friends, we will realize that our struggles are the same as those of others, and this makes us see that our problems are not unique. Others may also be going through similar situations.

Having emotional problems is normal. "You know, it happened to me too once" is the common response when we share what is happening to us. We can then pray together for a specific issue, which makes us emotionally and spiritually stronger.

God also speaks to us through other people. Many times God's revelation to people comes through interactions and experiences with others. This is why we can say that good friendships generate good health.

As for mutual help relationships, we have a good definition in Galatians 6:2, where Paul advises, *"Carry each other's burdens, and in this way you will fulfill the law of Christ."* This is one of the greatest benefits of relationships: being willing to provide help when someone needs it and being able to ask for help if needed. Through meaningful relationships we can show care and spend time in celebration, communication, and emotional expression. It is good to talk and share with others. When someone feels understood, listened to, and supported, they feel calmer, contained, and their burden is relieved. Relationships give back to us, and spending time with loved friends and family generates health. Sorrows are relieved with someone understands us, and social relationships can generate a healthy biological and emotional response. One of the pillars of strength through problems and illness is strong relationships with other people.

Having emotional problems is normal.

Clearly, the Bible recognizes that the people we associate with have a great influence on us (since relationships can either heal or harm our lives) and strongly warns against associating with those who disobey God and avoiding relationship with them. Proverbs 22:24-25 advises us, *"Do not make friends with a hot-tempered person, do not associate with one easily angered, or you may learn their ways and get yourself ensnared."* It tells us that being with others who do wrong leads to learning from them to do wrong.

We are also instructed to avoid the foolish: *"Walk with the wise and become wise, for a companion of fools suffers harm"* (Proverbs 13:20). This is particularly critical in certain stages of life such as adolescence, when there is a tendency to imitate the behavior of others, seeking approval and group membership. During adolescence, there are many social influences on behavior, which is why it is so important to be aware of the friendships adolescents form.

All people need closeness with others. It is good to avoid loneliness. Each of us should pay attention to feelings of loneliness or isolation in ourselves. Feelings of loneliness and social isolation contribute to many mental health problems. For pastors and leaders, good places to make connections are pastoral councils and peer groups, conferences, and Christian retreats. Pray that the Lord will guide you to contact the right people, and make yourself available and open to new encounters. Proverbs 18:24 tells us that *"There are friends who bring us to ruin, but there are friends more faithful than a brother."*

Paul had very close relationships: In Colossians 4, he says that Aristarchus, Mark, and Justus helped, encouraged, and strengthened him. His network also included Luke, Timothy, Gaius, and Onesimus. In 2 Corinthians 7: 6-7, we read: "*...God, who comforts the downcast, comforted us by the coming of Titus, and not only by his coming but also by the comfort you had given him. He told us about your longing for me, your deep sorrow, your ardent concern for me, so that my joy was greater than ever.*" When Paul was distressed, he says that God comforted him with the arrival of Titus and that his presence was a joy in times of depression.

In serving the Lord, we connect with many people, and these relationships generally produce concern and tiredness. Ministering through inner healing, praying, advising, pointing out sins, healing wounds, interceding, preventing, warning, guiding, etc.—all these tasks wear us out and drain our energy and strength. When you feel this way, try taking a break to call a friend or colleague to talk and share. That brief interaction will make a difference in how you feel. Make sure to commit to regular contact with others, beyond the people you contact for your work or ministry. The quality of the people you connect with makes a difference. Avoid toxic relationships or those that violate your personal boundaries and make sure to connect with people who enrich and nurture you.

Analyze if there are walls built up toward others due to past negative experiences, and if there are, tear them down.

12. Creativity and mental health

Creativity is the ability to generate new ideas or concepts that produce original solutions. Is there any problem, conflict, or painful situation that you feel you will never be able to resolve? Is there any emotional or mental illness that paralyze you, that you feel you have no resources to face? Have you resigned yourself to living through a difficult situation thinking that you will have to endure it for the rest of your life? Has the phrase "This has no solution; this will never end" appeared in your mind? If you answer yes to these questions, you are probably experiencing what is called paralysis in thought. Thought paralysis leads you to always see things in the same way, to convince yourself that things are that way and will never change, and to stop acting in situations where you should make important decisions to solve your problem.

Creativity can be used to overcome the past and to think about problems in a different way, given that there are other resources available in the present.

Have you ever given a new meaning to a negative situation from the past that still disturbs you today? Creativity can lead us to leave the usual paths and seek new approaches and behaviors.

Creativity in this sense means learning different alternatives in how to act. Many times people are not aware of how bad things are, or they have gotten used to their difficulties; seeing the problem and wanting to change it is already an act of creativity.

Creativity can also be beneficial in giving a new meaning to traumatic situations of the past, such as an unresolved loss, the breakup of a family relationship, or even abuse, which continue to influence and generate fear, resentment, or pain. Creativity can be used to overcome the past, to approach the problem in a different way; it can lead to new understanding, given that in the present there are other resources available and a more complete view of the problem can be obtained.

One way to view a difficult situation in a different light is to talk about the problem with someone who knows how to listen. When people start to recount their past experiences, new ideas usually emerge. This results in shedding light on the reason behind certain feelings that still exist in the present and giving a different meaning to the past. One we know of is a 26-year-old woman who had been abused as a child by a family member. She struggled with depression and still lived with guilt and fear. After working through this pain with a Christian psychologist, she expressed the realization that she was not to blame for what happened.

In the Bible are stories showing that even God is willing to change His way of thinking, to be creative in the face of a new reality. There are instances where God modified His sentences or decrees based on people's response to His messages.

God is creative, and as vessels of clay, we are constantly being molded by Him. Our brains are constantly being shaped by our environment and life experiences, which, if negative, can give rise to many mental health issues.

We should understand that all experiences—even the most painful or difficult ones—can lead to the development of our character. The Bible encourages us to find joy in going through different trials, as they can produce in us a steadfastness and maturity, without lacking anything. In the Bible we see examples that can encourage us to believe that after suffering for a little while, God Himself will restore, strengthen, and establish us.

In a class on character development I taught for a period at the Buenos Aires Bible Institute, I asked students to share an experience from their lives that had influenced the development of their character. Many of them shared stories with sad or painful content and described how difficult the situation had been for them—which, despite the negative burden, had been very helpful to their personal growth. They described these experiences as learning opportunities that had formed positive aspects of their character and taught them valuable lessons.

13. Familial environment and mental health

Each family has an emotional climate generated by the interaction of its members. The family environment impacts each member of the family, generating health or illness.

What is the reason for this?

The brain is like plastic: It can adapt to changes through its neural networks. A dendritic spine, which is a connection to another neuron, can be created in twenty seconds, meaning that there is a brain change that comes with new learning, a new experience lived. This capacity is enormous in the early years, but continues throughout life. We have a flexible brain, and all these stimuli are integrated into the mind, generating our way of being and acting.

The family environment and the experiences we live within our families impact our minds, influence us, permeate us, and can generate positive or negative stimuli. The brain is shaped in relation to the environment and life experiences that, if negative, can give rise to many mental illnesses.

Every human being is a product of their genome, but perhaps to a greater extent, they are a product of the experiences they live throughout their life. That is to say, the set of experiences makes that human being a unique and unrepeatable individual. We cannot control the environment our children live in at school, nor the one in our work or in our country, but we can control the environment in our home, which has a very large influence on our and our children's mental health.

There is a phrase that can help us understand the mind: Everything that is stimulated develops.

There's a phrase that can help us understand the mind: Everything that is stimulated develops. Receiving and having received love, containment, and support from childhood generates good self-esteem. The positive emotional bond that the child develops with their parents of being accepted and unconditionally protected, provides the essential emotional security for a good development of personality. If, instead, children have suffered traumas that generate vulnerability, this can lead to multiple possible paths of illness(2).

Health is generated in our homes and communities by:

- The treatment among its members. Matthew 7:12 tells us, *"Do to others whatever you would like them to do to you. This is the essence of all that is taught in the law and the prophets."*
- Love and expressions of love among its members. In 1 Thessalonians 3:12 we read, *"May the Lord make your love increase and overflow for each other and for everyone else..."*
- Communication among its members. Ephesians 4:29 teaches us, *"Do not let any unwholesome talk come out of your mouths, but only what is helpful for building others up according to their needs, that it may benefit those who listen."*

- The presence of praise and gratitude to God. In Habakkuk 3:17-18 we read, "*Though the fig tree does not bud and there are no grapes on the vines, though the olive crop fails and the fields produce no food, though there are no sheep in the pen and no cattle in the stalls, yet I will rejoice in the Lord, I will be joyful in God my Savior.*"

Chapter 7

The impact of the pandemic on mental health.

Even as Christians, we are vulnerable to the unforeseen consequences and aftermath of the pandemic. This unpredictable and challenging global reality has impacted the lives of many people and families.

> **The uncertainty and fear brought about by the pandemic have caused emotional problems for the majority of people.**

In this final chapter, we attempt to analyze the consequences and possible solutions to some of the problems that the pandemic has left within the family sphere. The aftermath that we will consider next has led us to question things like: How do we take care of ourselves and each other? What resources do we have? How do we care for, support, and help in the midst of pain?

What is the reality of the post-pandemic, and how do we move forward?

I. Consequences for Individuals and Families

Mental Health Disorders

The lockdown and fear of the pandemic brought emotional problems to the vast majority of people. There was an increase in mood disorders and anxiety disorders in the general population (as described in Chapter 4), along with heightened feelings of insecurity, uncertainty, nervousness, despair, helplessness, vague fears, specific fears, and panic, among others.

Interpersonal relationships were disrupted, with a tendency toward isolation and withdrawal. Families living in confined spaces for extended periods experienced intolerance and violent behavior among their members. Due to job loss, economic hardship, and loss of loved ones, many people suffered from depression, loss of self-esteem, a lack of self-worth, and feelings of hopelessness, doubt, and unanswered questions. Emotional fatigue and difficulty concentrating were also common.

There was an increase in alcohol, hypnotic, and drug consumption. Children, specifically due to the lockdown and prolonged school closures, experienced a lack of social interaction with their peers and developmental delays.

Emotional Fatigue

Emotional fatigue is a state of chronic physical and psychological exhaustion due to excessive personal demands and prolonged stress, resulting in feelings of emotional exhaustion and depletion.

Many Christians typically engage in acts of helping the community and their faith family out of love and empathy for those who are suffering. However, during the pandemic, many of them went to great lengths to help others, such as buying and preparing food, staying in constant online contact to inquire about their well-being, praying, and providing counsel. Over time, these Christians experienced emotional fatigue, displaying symptoms such as tiredness, burnout, deep-seated feelings of weariness and disinterest, heightened levels of stress leading to feelings of alarm and anxiety. They became excessively cautious to avoid infection, experienced difficulty sleeping, and struggled with memory and clear thinking (referred to as «brain fog» due to attention deficit). Other cognitive symptoms of emotional fatigue include difficulty with verbal fluency, decreased thinking speed, categorization problems, and memory issues, among others.

This indicates that while it is true that, as children of God, we should bear one another's burdens, we also need to recognize our personal limitations

This indicates that while it is true that, as children of God, we should bear one another's burdens, we also need to recognize our personal limitations, set appropriate boundaries, and take care of ourselves, as well as those who care for the needy, as excessive burdens can have negative consequences for mental health.

Emotional Stagnation

We have seen that, in the context of the pandemic, many people have experienced emotional stagnation, leading to a fear of making decisions. People have suffered from the impact of abrupt changes in their environment and from the excess of information they received through the media. Daily reports of infections and deaths, financial losses of large and small businesses, job losses of family and friends, etc., have emotionally paralyzed people. They are unable to decide on their own situation and needs, and cannot analyze the situation because they are always spinning around the same issues. In addition, the Infodemic, which is the epidemic of information generated around COVID-19 and its devastating consequences, created an excess of analysis trying to figure out how to act and what was best, which complicated the decision-making process. Many people were mentally and emotionally exhausted.

Consequences of the Pandemic on the Elderly

Working with the elderly, as we are a geriatrician (Daniel) and a psycho gerontologist (Elida), we have noticed an acceleration of the aging process at a physical and emotional level in older adults. Physically, symptoms such as increased hair loss, more wrinkles due to increased skin dryness, an abrupt decrease in flexibility and deterioration of muscle strength, weight gain, and slower walking have been observed. Psychologically, there was an increase in depressive symptoms.

Remaining active despite chronological age leads to healthy aging.

Socially, the pandemic and the fear of contagion forced the elderly to stay at home, advised not to even go to the supermarket or take a walk to get some sunlight. They lost the necessary social contact at this stage of life, already characterized by isolation. Gyms were closed, elderly centers were shut down, and all group physical activities and workshops for the elderly were suspended, through which active aging is promoted. Outings, excursions, and trips for the elderly were also canceled, and all of these are opportunities that stimulate the continuity of psychophysical activity and promote and facilitate the initiation of new personal bonds.

Remaining active despite chronological age leads to healthy aging. However, because of the pandemic, none of this could be done. For this reason, the vast majority abandoned their professional and commercial activities that they were still carrying out despite being retired; others abandoned the academic activities they had started to sustain and occupy their free time from responsibilities, and the start of new projects and ventures was also abandoned. This led to an increase in emotions and feelings such as sadness, unease, loss of interest, emotional disconnection, and apathy—all symptoms of advanced old age.

How can an older adult help themselves?

Firstly, consider that the way they see themselves says a lot about how they age. Secondly, take into account the loss of their own physical health and take care with medication for any chronic illnesses they may have. Thirdly, consider social losses, by helping themselves to overcome the loss of emotional ties, family members, friends, and church members, and by caring for and cultivating a social network of support, sustenance, and new friends. Fourth, maintain the ability to continue learning, and to project themselves with new goals and activities. Fifthly, take care of the place where they live, making it pleasant and suitable for their needs. And lastly—but not least—maintain positive affections with friends, family, and especially within their marriage.

Grieving for Many Loved Ones Who Died During the Pandemic

Another consequence of the pandemic that affected the emotional health of families is that many people died due to the arrival of the epidemic and the lack of resources of all kinds to cope with it. The pandemic has left widows and orphans in many families who were enveloped in grief, going through a time of mourning for the loss of their loved ones. Understanding the biblical phrase «Blessed are those who mourn» in this context becomes very difficult for many, but the rest of the sentence that follows says «for they will be comforted,» and this truly fills the grieving heart with hope. During the mourning process, one receives from the Lord a special hope, a timely grace, a unique and singular comfort that only He can give to heal the wounds of the heart. In these times, the words of Psalm 146:9 come true, which says: *«The Lord (...) cares for the orphan and the widow (...),»* and of Psalm 68:5: *«He is the father of the fatherless; he ensures justice for the widows, he is God in his holy dwelling.»*

We will try to answer two questions: (a) How can we help ourselves if a loved one has passed away? and (b) How can we help those who have lost a loved one?

How do we help ourselves?

Perhaps you have lost a loved one recently. There have been many losses, and what you are experiencing is more than just a passing storm—it is a tornado or a destructive earthquake for which there was no warning. When this happens, the normal reaction is tears and crying as expressions of pain. These expressions have nothing to do with a lack of faith, are not pathological, and do not require medication; tears are part of the normal reaction to loss and not only are they legitimate but also desirable. It is even possible to think of them as a form of protection against depression: when a person is sad and cries, they may actually be recovering from a painful storm, such as the death of a loved one; so they cry, but without losing faith.

In times of such pain, it is good to identify the causes of your crying. All causes are valid for crying.

In times of such pain, it is good to identify the causes of your crying. All causes are valid for crying. During the grieving process, there are moments when one cries for the person who passed away, thinking that they can no longer enjoy this or that thing; there are other moments when one cries for the pain that the children have for the loss of their father, for example, and other moments when one cries because they can no longer count on the deceased to share or do countless things that they used to do together. One cries for loneliness, for the irreversibility of death. It is very difficult to navigate the pain of losing a loved one, but it is even more difficult in solitude. If this is your case, the recommendation is not to be alone; seek help and surround yourself with faithful people who can accompany you in this process and help you sustain your faith in our Lord.

We all know that in this world we will have affliction, and yet the process of grieving is difficult for us as Christians, but the following phrase: «*In the world, you will have tribulation. But take heart; I have overcome the world*» (John 16:33, RVR1960) gives us relief. Thank you, Lord! We say this to you, as we have experienced grief over the loss of our beautiful and beloved 24-year-old daughter, a pain that continues to be felt even after several years have passed, and having reached the final stage of the grieving process,which is acceptance. The Lord pours out a special covering that falls upon the faithful Christian going through such pain, providing special strength; He pours out an incredible spiritual oil that softens the pain of the wound, a special grace that is an ability that God grants to us to fulfill His will. It is a manifestation of the Holy Spirit, a special and unique covering that falls upon the Christian going through the pain of losing a loved one, providing them with special and unexplainable strength.

Our Lord is the God of all comfort, His promises renew our strength and console us in our pain. Psalm 119:114 says: «*You are my hiding place and my shield; I hope in your word.*» God always gives comfort to His beloved children when they suffer. God gives grace to endure suffering; it is good to see suffering as a life experience, as a time of growth to move forward in life. It is also a time to continue to grow in our relationship with God, to continue to trust in Him despite everything, to always stand firm in the Lord. *«Let us hold fast the confession of our hope without wavering, for He who promised is faithful»* (Hebrews 10:23).

The time of grieving is a time to cry and seek refuge in the Lord, to read the Psalms, pray, and express feelings of pain with sincerity, and to express alongside the Psalmist your heart-wrenching complaints, your unanswered questions, and your confused emotions, always trusting in the Lord, the owner of your life. In the Psalms, we not only find the promises that bless and strengthen us, but we also find a great expression of both sweet and bitter feelings. You can be honest with the Lord, He knows your heart, He understands you, and He also feels your pain.

How do we take care of our emotions and help ourselves?

To have a healthy mind and maintain mental health, it is advisable to accept reality, allow yourself the necessary time to go through all stages of grief, listen to and respect the normal imbalances of emotional states during the process, listen to and take care of the body, be honest with ourselves and with the Lord in prayer, without denying or avoiding the feelings of our grieving heart. We understand the disciples because, like us, they found themselves unexpectedly in an unmanageable situation when they were in the boat in the middle of the storm while Jesus slept. Their fear was to sink in the storm. Sometimes it seems like Jesus is asleep while we struggle in the midst of the storm, not hearing a response to our prayers, but no, Jesus is in the boat with us, He never leaves us, He knows all things and has control over them. Faith in Him helps us to hold on until the storm passes, and it is there where we will see the power of the Lord, when the stormy situation is restored, even when we live in a new reality.

A healing concept is to accept the new reality, even if we never wanted it. Accepting does not mean approving, in the sense of qualifying the event that caused suffering as good and positive. Accepting does not mean resentful resignation to what cannot be avoided; accepting means integrating the loss into one's own life, which is very painful but healthy.

A healing concept is to accept the new reality, even if we never wanted it.

How do we help those who have lost a loved one?

These are times to learn to accompany others in grief, to empathize with the suffering of others, and to put into practice «mourning with those who mourn.» It's a time to help each other in a different way—a time of consolation.

The best approach is to accompany them, show love in every possible way, and respect what they express, even if it's confusing, misguided, or wrong, and provide help and care. Offer to help with whatever they need—at home, with children, with errands and shopping, whatever; not to teach what is already known, much less to sermonize or judge; just listen, surround them with love, and above all, pray for them a lot. Recognize and respect their feelings, the emotions expressed, and their unbalanced moods. Respect their crying, their laughter, their silences; do not expect more than they can give or do, and do not demand. Respect their timing, do not leave them alone, do not forget about them or their pain, and connect frequently—ask how they are, what they need, and tell them that we are praying for them. Assure them that, even in this new reality, life is worth living, that their lives are hidden in Christ, that the Lord is always present and can and wants to help them. Affirm the truth that God never punishes with illness and death, and that nothing will separate them from God's unconditional love; that they are loved by Him and that He never abandoned them. Life holds many unanswered questions, but as Matthew 28:20 says, *«(...) And surely I am with you always, to the very end of the age.»*

2. Economic Problems

The economic problems have left many families with greater economic instability, impossible debts to pay off, and a lack of resources to cover basic family needs. Economic problems have triggered many negative feelings, and hopelessness has taken over many families. Job loss has led to the question: What are we going to do now? Economic crises have a negative impact on family health, bringing uncertainty, insecurity, and fear of losing stability.

Stress is an anxiety disorder. When a person suffers from anxiety, they turn any situation into a catastrophic event.

Economic problems deteriorate the education of children and destroy family hopes, exacerbating mood crises. Unemployment heightens latent problems in families; dissatisfaction leads to irritability, uncertainty brings unease, and a lack of food and essential products produces fear and desperation. Lack of tolerance is expressed through anger, resentment, and hostility.

The loss of employment leads to personal devaluation, feelings of failure, and a lack of personal worth. A decrease in self-esteem and lack of recognition generates stress, which manifests through anxiety. If economic problems persist without finding a solution, they can lead to psychosomatic problems such as neck pain, dizziness, tremors, high cholesterol, strokes, etc., which are the product of chronic stress. These problems carry a burden of anguish and hopelessness that the body resents.

Stress is an anxiety disorder. When a person suffers from anxiety, they transform any situation into a catastrophic event: if their chest hurts, they think they're having a heart attack; if their stomach hurts, they fantasize about an ulcer, and this happens because fear causes them to focus on their own body when in reality, the cause of the anxiety lies in the economic problem, because the strongest stressor is uncertainty, especially in the job field. Those who have a family and no job suffer a lot of anguish.

3. Marital Problems

The pandemic left three different outcomes in the lives of families: marital break-ups, marriages in crisis, and marriages that have grown.

Marital Break-Ups

Health, emotional, and economic problems revealed the fragility of many marital relationships. Many conflicts that were hidden by the routine and lack of interaction among family members before the pandemic came to light; the time of the pandemic confined families, in many cases, in restricted environments, with bored or uncontrollable children, and fearful and worried adults. The frustration of confinement brought about increased self-absorption, and everything increased intolerance, irritability, domestic, verbal, and physical violence, which caused difficult wounds to heal. Old fights and resentments gave rise to a number of unpleasant and disturbing feelings of discomfort that led to greater disagreements and misunderstandings, which then led to separations and divorces. The divorce and separation rate increased, as did requests for psychiatric treatment. Marriages destroyed by broken relationships brought an uncertain future for many children, who experienced dizzying and baffling changes, and all these events caused an increase in the number of people suffering in solitude.

Marriages in Crisis

Many other marriages did not end in divorce, but are suffering the consequences of destructive behaviors or decisions in their relationship and in their own lives, experiencing the symptoms of emotional disorders. Shouting increases blood pressure and heart rate; in fights, it's like the heart jumps out of the mouth. Stress levels cause damage to the brain and emotions, and anxiety appears with mood swings and hostility. They need help. We read in Isaiah 61:4 the following: «*They will rebuild the ancient ruins and restore the places long devastated [...],*» and in 1 Corinthians 1:10, this: «*I appeal to you, brothers and sisters, in the name of our Lord Jesus Christ, that all of you agree with one another in what you say and that there be no divisions among you, but that you be perfectly united in mind and thought.*»

Emotions during the pandemic became disordered, and many were broken. For this reason, repair and reconstruction work is necessary.

The work of these couples is to repair what is destroyed between them, to put in order what is disordered in order to learn not to argue, and to live in harmony and unity. Emotions during the pandemic became disordered, and many were broken, so a work of repair and reconstruction is necessary. Cracks appeared in people; they were damaged, hurt, and there were emotional holes that needed to be repaired, just like a mason repairs cracked walls and rebuilds what is crumbling. This is God's task—He can and wants to do it—but we must give Him space and allow Him to work in each person and in the bond that unites them in marriage.

It is also the task of each person to work to strengthen the emotional bond that keeps them together. They must decide to take care of each other, love each other more and better, and take care of the relationship. They should dedicate time to personal growth, maturation, and change; time to forgive, respect, and accept themselves and each other as they are; and to love themselves with their qualities, virtues, and flaws. They also need time to learn to communicate more and better, to decide to recover the affectionate dialogue they once had, and to develop constructive communication with their children and restore broken family relationships. This is a time to be wise, to repair mistakes, and to build new ways of relating, to resist tensions and problems in order to remain firm and united. It is a time to pray to the Lord for a renewed love in marriage.

It is often said that a time of crisis is a time of opportunities, and a time of uncertainty is also a time full of possibilities. God can turn things around, and problems often become, in due time, a source of blessing for you and your family. In times of crisis and pain, it is good to pray a lot and even cry in the presence of the Lord in those moments of spiritual intimacy.

In Isaiah 28:12, God says, «*They would find rest in their own land if they would obey God and be generous and good. That is what the Lord told them.*» We can successfully navigate pandemics and post-pandemics, crises, problems, and suffering if we listen to the Lord, look to others, and maintain a Christian character. If we learn to live in His rest, in obedience, and if we act with kindness and generosity, He will give us the necessary strength to focus with determination on what God is calling us to do. We read, «*Therefore I tell you, whatever you ask for in prayer, believe that you have received it, and it will be yours*» (Mark 11:24). Hebrews 11:1 also says: «*Now faith is confidence in what we hope for and assurance about what we do not see.*» James 1:6 adds, «*But when you ask, you must believe and not doubt, because the one who doubts is like a wave of the sea, blown and tossed by the wind.*» Finally, Jesus tells His disciples that with enough faith, even what is considered impossible can be done by the power of His name: «*Truly I tell you, if you have faith as small as a mustard seed, you can say to this mountain, 'Move from here to there,' and it will move. Nothing will be impossible for you»* (Matthew 17:20, NIV).

Marriages that Have Grown

It is also worth mentioning that there are a significant number of marriages that, thanks to the lockdown of the quarantine, have dedicated more time to converse, dialogue, and be intimate. They found each other in a different way, the distance between them shortened, they took the time to address pending situations, and reached agreements that blessed their relationship and their lives. Their love became enriched, their emotional bond matured, and they emerged stronger from the pandemic. They enjoyed their children more, and we see that these marriages that reorganized their time were the most effective in organizing their day: upon waking up, they had a moment for breakfast; then they had different moments—conversations, playing with their children, praying together, reading together or separately, having time alone, singing as a family, eating, enjoying television, and much more. Having the day divided into scheduled moments to follow helped them plan their days and reduced the anxiety of thinking, «What are we going to do now?»

Three Resources

We will explore three concepts that can help us: wisdom, flexibility, and God's kairos.

We need wisdom to feel strong in this new time. We know that the Lord has plans for each of His children, as Jeremiah 29:11 says: *«For I know the plans I have for you, declares the Lord, plans for welfare and not for evil, to give you a future and a hope.»* His plans are always good for our lives and families. We put God's plans into practice by making correct and wise decisions, for which we need wisdom.

The source of the wisdom we receive comes from above, which is the spiritual discernment that only God can give. Psalm 32:8 says, «*I will instruct you and teach you in the way you should go.*» He tells us that He will give us wisdom to undertake and show us what the right decisions are according to His will.

The keys to making the right decisions are dependence and obedience by faith in the Lord, and guidance is found in Proverbs 24:3-6: «*By wisdom a house is built, and by understanding it is established; by knowledge the rooms are filled with all precious and pleasant riches. A wise man is full of strength, and a man of knowledge enhances his might. For by wise guidance you can wage your war, and in abundance of counselors there is victory.*»

Wisdom: We need wisdom, which we can ask the Lord for, and He gives it without reproach, as we read in Proverbs 2:6: «*For the Lord gives wisdom; from His mouth come knowledge and understanding,*» and in James 1:5: «*If any of you lacks wisdom, you should ask God, who gives generously to all without finding fault.*» Wisdom gives the ability to build things, engage in activities, perform tasks, and carry out work.

The source of the wisdom we receive comes from above, which is the spiritual discernment that only God can give.

Intelligence: Intelligence generates new ideas and proposals, enabling creativity to reinvent itself, create new plans and projects, and make decisions with creative thoughts and new ideas, and act with good judgment, making the most suitable decisions without fear or uncertainty in implementing them.

Knowledge: Knowledge is what is learned through study. Training helps to expand and build ideas and thoughts, and to better understand necessary aspects to apply in the workplace. With greater knowledge, the ability to solve problems improves, raising self-esteem and creating new opportunities.

Power: «The wise person has more power.» Wisdom gives power, and power gives authority to dominate situations. Power is the ability to develop new ventures and generate courage, which instills self-confidence in what one knows and can do, facing the fear of failure and making mistakes.

Strategy: Strategy is a set of carefully planned and organized measures and actions to carry out a purpose or achieve a specific goal. Strategy is the ability to see available possibilities and create an action plan to undertake or resolve matters with prudence, haste, and without hesitation. The best strategy is to seek advice, as «in the multitude of counselors there is wisdom.»

Victory is achieved with many advisors, so having a good strategy before making a decision and embarking on something new is to seek advice.

Flexibility: Crises are overcome with flexibility. To help ourselves and others in the face of problems and to make decisions, flexibility is required, which is the capacity to adapt to the changes that circumstances demand. Perhaps, to overcome the aforementioned problems, now is the time to make decisions and necessary changes that will bring growth to the marital relationship. Maybe in the workplace, it is time to embark on something new or to implement new ways of managing time, effort, and money. Flexibility arises from the ability to recognize what you are capable of doing. Recognizing the abilities and gifts that you have been given by God can be used for new ventures.

Here, emotions can be helpful or a hindrance. Fear and doubts paralyze, uncertainty and self-devaluation stop you, but desire, enthusiasm, and motivation invigorate. The necessary energy is generated to use the capabilities that you already have and seek out new options and possibilities to undertake them with creative ideas. The motivated person continues to desire, dream, and think of new alternatives; new strength is awakened and fatigue disappears. With the capacity for work, courage, effort, and perseverance, the plan is achieved.

God's Kairos in the Pandemic

Kairos is the time of opportunity. It can be a time of waiting, a set time, the right, opportune, suitable, and just time; it is the time that can change our destiny. In the New Testament, kairos is used more than eighty times and each time it is to express the «when» of God, the God of eternity: *«My times are in your hands»* (Psalms 31:15 RVR1960).

1 Thessalonians 5:1 says, *«Brothers and sisters, you do not need anything written to you about the times and dates.»* This text shows us that we have to pay attention to God's kairos, a difficult time where all our spiritual senses must await the manifestations of God.

Be wise in managing your time, to avoid episodes of stress, anxiety, or distress that can make you sick; this depends on you, and so you will have more opportunities to take advantage of God's kairos in your life, the timely and designed time from heaven, where God will intervene in a supernatural and powerful way. The pandemic can be the opportune time for the purpose that God had prepared or planned in advance for you to be fulfilled in your life. We read in Ephesians 2:10 that *«we are God's handiwork, created in Christ Jesus to do good works, which God prepared in advance for us to do.»* It is time to recognize that your life has a purpose and you are a unique design of God, with your own potential and attributes; it is also time to believe in your own abilities and overcome negative attitudes, self-destructive thoughts that threaten to settle in and paralyze the future. It is time to overcome the fall of self-esteem that the pandemic left behind; God gave you the means to be and do what He wants you to do, for example, to do good work in this time that has already been prepared by God in advance.

Be wise in managing your time, to avoid episodes of stress, anxiety, or distress that can make you sick

They stop and paralyze, because now is the time to rebuild what has been dismantled and broken, to build another project with new and renewed strength. It is time to encourage yourself and others to undertake, to let go of the past and look forward, time to learn to manage the resources of time, effort, and money, time for cooperation, to support each other as a family towards a common family goal, to start something together in the workplace, learning to help, value, and encourage each other, discarding devaluation and all types of aggression and destructive competition, to join efforts for the good of all.

It is time to recognize that it is possible, because strength comes from God. We read in Philippians 4:13: «*I can do all things through Christ who strengthens me.*» It is time to recognize that you have gifts, talents, abilities, and qualities given by God for you to develop while you live, and you must thank God for that.

Wisdom gives you the «what,» flexibility gives you the «how,» and God's kairos gives you the «when.» With God, we have everything!

With a renewed love in marriage and family, and a deep intimacy with the Lord, with the wisdom that comes from God, flexibility put into action, and knowing God's kairos, difficulties and economic problems can be endured and faced, and embark on a new path looking towards the future with hope.

Appendix I

A brief description of the role of healthcare professionals and agents in the field of mental health

Psychiatrist

A psychiatrist is a doctor specialized in the field of mental health. They are responsible for preventing, diagnosing, and treating mental, emotional, and behavioral disorders, and implementing appropriate treatments. They are qualified to prescribe medication, provide advice, and prescribe suitable drugs, taking into account their therapeutic effects, undesirable side effects, or possible interactions with other medications the person may be taking. They conduct medication monitoring and adjustments, as well as the evaluation and follow-up of treatments.

Neurologist

A neurologist is a physician who specializes in diseases that affect the central nervous system and the neuromuscular system. This means they deal with all conditions affecting both the brain and the nerves and muscles of the nervous system. Some of the most common conditions they treat are headaches or migraines, Alzheimer's disease, Parkinson's disease, multiple sclerosis, epilepsy, stroke, and tumors. During a consultation, they perform a physical examination and may order or perform necessary additional tests (such as brain scans or magnetic resonance imaging) to arrive at an accurate diagnosis.

Psychologist

A psychologist is a qualified professional who has received formal university training in psychology. The degree typically takes four or five years to complete (depending on the curriculum of each university), and upon completion, they obtain a psychology degree. Psychologists study human behavior, including issues related to learning, thought processes, emotions, and behaviors, both in their normal development and in various disorders or problems. They also perform psycho diagnostics through structured and unstructured interviews and the administration of a battery of tests. Psycho diagnostics aim to assess the mental health status of the person seeking help and are crucial in guiding appropriate treatment. The evaluation covers different areas of the patient's psychological functioning (affective, cognitive, and relational) and attempts to define the personality traits and conflicts underlying the reason for the consultation.

Counselor

A counselor is a professional in counseling whose work focuses on personal development and utilizing individuals' potential. They do not deal with mental illnesses. Counseling is aimed at individuals who need a listening ear and support to better understand their problems and facilitate their resolution, make decisions, or make changes in certain aspects of their lives. Their work is primarily in institutional settings. In Argentina, counseling is a two-year technical tertiary-level career, with classes attended both virtually and in person three times a week.

Therapeutic Companion

In Argentina, this is a two-year undergraduate program aimed at providing assistance and support to chronic or acute patients, either in their homes or in mental health institutions. The therapeutic companion is a healthcare assistant who provides personalized home care to individuals with mental illness and their families. One of their roles is to provide support to patients during times of crisis. Depending on the situation, they may accompany the patient in their home for short or extended periods of time. In some cases, they assist the patient with daily activities that they may not be able to carry out on their own. One of their functions is to identify the remaining traces of willpower in their patients and use them as a source of energy to move forward.

It is also common for therapeutic companions to encourage patients to continue with their treatment, especially when there are psychological issues that hinder therapy progress. The professional must be trained to help patients overcome emotional barriers, and another one of their roles is to enhance the patient's social relationships. They may encourage participation in games and recreational activities or even support them in undertaking work tasks. In essence, the therapeutic companion is the support system for the patient during their treatment. The goal is for the individual receiving support to improve their condition and acquire as much autonomy as possible, minimizing limitations and maximizing their abilities. Ultimately, once the treatment is completed, the person should have more resources to lead their life.

Pastoral Counseling

A significant percentage of Christians with emotional or mental problems will likely seek guidance from a pastor before approaching a professional. Pastoral counseling is when a pastor or leader provides spiritual discernment, advice, guidance, and assistance to individuals in resolving personal or relational conflicts. Pastors are called to counsel and determine when it is necessary to refer these cases to a professional in the field.

Christian counseling has been with us since biblical times. The Bible is filled with spiritually-minded men and women who have been used by God to encourage, guide, support, confront, advise, and help others in various ways. Jesus is described as the Wonderful Counselor, and His followers were taught to utilize God's Word for this purpose, as we read in 2 Timothy 3:16: *"All Scripture is God-breathed and is useful for teaching, rebuking, correcting, and training in righteousness."* As we can see, the primary tool of a Christian counselor is the Word of God, using its revealed truths. The Word of God *"is alive and active. Sharper than any double-edged sword, it penetrates even to divide soul and spirit, joints and marrow; it judges the thoughts and attitudes of the heart"* (Hebrews 4:12, NIV).

Pastoral counseling techniques depend largely on the pastor's personality and the nature of the issues being addressed. There is no one-size-fits-all approach to biblical counseling, just as there isn't for missions, evangelism, or preaching.

Inner Healing

Also known as healing of damaged emotions, healing of memories, or healing of wounded spirits. These names accurately describe what inner healing is about.

In 1 Thessalonians 5:23-24, we read, *"May God himself, the God of peace, sanctify you through and through. May your whole spirit, soul, and body be kept blameless at the coming of our Lord Jesus Christ. The one who calls you is faithful, and he will do it."*

This verse describes what inner healing means: sanctifying us as Christians and keeping our spirit and soul blameless. It speaks of an inner transformation, which is the process by which a person who has already accepted Christ as their Savior is freed and healed from wounds and traumas from past or present experiences.

Inner healing is the healing of painful or traumatic experiences. During this process, techniques are used to help individuals release bondage caused by unforgiveness. They are guided to forgive those who have hurt, betrayed, or have different types of debts with them, and to ask for forgiveness for their own faults and sins. This entails a transformation and renewal of the soul, will, emotions, and mind through the Word of God and the Holy Spirit. The revelation received during moments of healing is given by the Holy Spirit and the gifts of revelation. This process helps foster a grateful attitude, let go of guilt, sadness, and anger associated with past painful situations, as well as anxiety, despair, and lack of faith related to present circumstances, in order to believe in and trust God and tear down the walls that limit the power of the Holy Spirit

Appendix II

Medical conferences and scientific publications that refer to faith and spirituality are beneficial resources for mental health.

The concept of spirituality as a strength in facing mental illness has been gaining increasing importance in specialty conferences and scientific publications.

Conferences

Worldwide psychiatry conferences have included the topic of mental health and spirituality in their workshops or presentations, taking into account the positive influence of this area on the evolution of mental illnesses within the medical field.

The following conferences are some examples:

- AASM (Argentine Association of Mental Health) from October 20 to 22, 2021, in Buenos Aires (Argentina). One presentation was on the topic of mental health and spirituality.
- VII Regional Congress of the WFMH (World Federation of Mental Health). A thematic axis of the conferences was "Strategies and psychospiritual resources in times of pandemic," from which we highlight some of their considerations: "The study of spirituality in the field of health has allowed the development of solid scientific evidence. Understanding the integrity of the human being and the multiple dimensions of spirituality, various psychospiritual resources are presented as coping strategies in times of socio-sanitary crisis."
- I European Congress of Christian Anthropology and Mental Health Sciences, organized by the Universitat Abat Oliba CEU (Barcelona, Spain) on September 13 and 14, 2019. In a statement, the Universitat explained that the relationship between spirituality and mental health "has been a problematic aspect for a long time, and in the specific case of Christianity there has been for many decades a mutual rejection that has hindered the integration of the principles of Christian anthropology with the foundations and practices of psychology. Christianity and psychology have turned their backs on each other for a long time."
- At the World Congress of Mental Health held in Buenos Aires (Argentina) from November 5 to 8, 2019, one of the thematic axes was mental health and spirituality. An evangelical pastor presented there.
- At the XXVII Argentine Congress of Mental Health organized by APSA (Argentine Association of Psychiatrists), one

of the thematic axes of the congress chapters was Psychiatry and Spirituality.

- The General Directorate of Research of the Antonio Ruiz de Montoya University (Peru) held the Fourth Research Week 2021 - Memory, transformation, and commitment. On the third day, the question "Is spirituality a relevant topic for mental health?" was presented.[1]
- From September 26 to 28, 2014, the V Congress of Anthropology, Psychology, and Spirituality organized by the Edith Stein Chair of the University of Mysticism (Ávila, Spain) took place. This time, the congress was titled "From victims to survivors," referring to the process of overcoming and personal growth that comes with surviving a traumatic event.
- At the XXXIX Brazilian Congress of Psychiatry from October 5 to 8, 2022, one of the thematic axes was Psychiatry and Spirituality.

Scientific Publications

In recent times, countless studies have been published regarding the benefit of faith and religious practices in the evolution of mental illnesses. Many scientific publications, faced with the difficulty of measuring a person's level of faith and spirituality when dealing with a mental illness, took different variables and indicators to elaborate it indirectly, quantifying behaviors and actions through questionnaires. These included:

- Frequency of attending church or religious services
- Active membership in the church
- Level of commitment and sense of belonging expressed
- Amount of time dedicated to prayer

1. ¿Es la espiritualidad un tema relevante para la salud mental? (Is spirituality a relevant issue for mental health?) Universidad Antonio Ruiz de Montoya - https://bit.ly/3Ab2bJP

- Frequency of reading sacred texts
- Number of decisions made according to their faith
- Whether their purpose in life and goals are related to spirituality
- Fear of death
- Hope for eternal life
- In a large number of these publications, the conclusions are very interesting; some of them include:
- People who engage in religious practices could increase their life expectancy by up to seven years[2]
- The fourth edition of the DSM (Diagnostic and Statistical Manual of Mental Disorders) recognizes spirituality as a relevant source of support for emotional distress.[3]
- In the U.S., in 1994, only three medical schools included spirituality in their curriculum; in 1997, this number increased to 30.
- A study of 91,000 subjects in Maryland found a lower prevalence of cirrhosis, emphysema, suicide, and ischemic heart disease in people who regularly attended their respective place of religious worship.[4]
- Studies like Damianakis (2012) claim that there is a positive correlation between a person›s spiritual dimension and their ability to adapt to the grief of losing a spouse.[5]

---

2. Hummer, R. A., Rogers, R. G., Nam, C. B., Ellison, C. G. Religious involvement and U.S. adult mortality. Demography, 1999; 36: 273-85. Helm, H. M., Hays, J. C., Flint, E. P., Koenig, H. G., Blazer, D. G. Does private religious activity prolong survival? A six-year follow-up study of 3,851 older adults. J Gerontol A Biol Sci Med Sci, 2000; 55: 400-5
3. La espiritualidad en la relación médico-paciente.(Spirituality in the doctor-patient relationship) intramed.net - https://bit.ly/3y3YFhO
4. Comstock, G. W., Partridge, K. B. Church attendance and health. J Chronic Dis, 1972; 25:665-72
5. Damianakis, T., Marziali E. Older adults" response to the loss of a spouse: the function of spirituality in understanding the grieving process. Aging Ment Health, 2012; 16(1):57-66

- Recently, low levels of depression and notable levels of general health were found in a study of elderly Koreans who had high levels of religiosity and spirituality.[6]
- Intercessory prayer has shown to be effective in reducing anxiety and increasing self-esteem.[7]
- It is argued that cognitive therapy based on religion has a favorable impact on Christian patients with depressive disorders.[8]
- Behaviors and attitudes based on religious beliefs, such as those related to smoking, drinking, physical exercise, or moderation in eating, can motivate health-promoting behaviors and reduce the risk of illness.[9]
- Faith would establish a mental structure that shapes a person›s ability to cope with health and illness. Thus, the cognitive style of a religious individual can provide a healthy mode of behavior in the face of pain, suffering, and other components associated with illnesses.[10]
- People who usually do not have religious ideas or practices may develop them times of crisis or illness, which is associated with the perception of a loss of personal control in the situation, leading them to seek a higher power or a god as a coping strategy.[11]

---

6. You K. S., Lee H. O., Fitzpatrick J. J., Kim, S., Marui, E., Lee, J. S. et al. Spirituality, depression, living alone, and perceived health among Korean older adults in the community. Arch
7. O›Laoire S. An experimental study of the effects of distant, intercessory prayer on self-esteem, anxiety, and depression. Altern Ther Health Med, 1997; 3: 38-53
8. Ostrom, R., Watkins, P., Dean, T., Mashburn, D. Comparative efficacy of religious and non-reli-gious individuals. J Consult Clin Psychol, 1992; 60: 94-103
9. Snyder, C. R. The past and possible futures of hope. J Soc Clin Psychol, 2000; 19: 11-28
10. Muris, P, De Jong, P. Monitoring and perception of threat. Pers Indiv Differ, 1993; 15: 467-70
11. Koenig, H. G. Religion, spirituality, and health: a review and update. Adv Mind Body Med.,2015; 29(3):19-22. 5. Moreira-Almeida, A., Koenig, H. G., Lucchetti, G. Clinical implications of spirituality to mental health: review of evidence and practical guidelines. Rev Bras Psiquiatr, 2014; 36:176-82

- Spirituality, religious activity, and prayer have been sources of comfort and stress relief for multitudes of people.[12]
- Seligman and Peterson speak of the positive psychological traits of individuals, identifying 24 character strengths or virtues that are present in all cultures worldwide. In their classification of human strengths and virtues, they consider spirituality, religiosity, and faith as a character strength. Believing that there is a universal purpose or meaning in the things that happen in the world and in one›s own existence, and believing that there is something greater that shapes and determines our behavior and protects us, is a character strength.[13]

All of this shows that even within the secular world, mental health professionals understand the importance of faith and religious beliefs for a better evolution of mental illnesses. Currently, being a believer or spirituality in general is valued as a factor of support and strength.

---

12. Wachholtz, A. B., Sambamthoori, U. National trends in prayer use as a coping mechanism for depression: changes from 2002 to 2007. J Relig Health, 2013; 52(4):1356-68. do:10.1007/ s10943-012-9649-y

13. Las 24 fortalezas personales. Martin Seligman - hittps://bit.ly/3npicPT

Reference Bibliography

Chapter 1

1. Battie, W., Monro, J. y otros. Los prolegómenos del tratamiento moral ("The prelude of moral treatment."), 2013, Editorial Pole-mos, Buenos Aires, pág. 307
2. Organización Mundial de la Salud - Preguntas más frecuentes (World Health Organization - Frequently Asked Questions) - https://bit.ly/39YCv8F
3. Sigerist, H., 1941
4. Dubos, R., 1995
5. Lalonde, Marc: El concepto de campo de la salud: una perspectiva canadiense. En: Promoción de la Salud: Una Antología (The concept of the health field: a Canadian perspective. In: Health Promotion: An Anthology), OPS-OMS, Washington, DC, Publicación Científica N° 557, Págs. 3-5, 1996
6. World Health Organization, Mental health: Strengthening our response Fact Sheet (2016)- https://bit.ly/3y3Yd35/
7. La salud mental en cifras (Mental health in figures) - Confederación Salud Mental España - https://bit.ly/3bE80KF
8. Moffitt, E. y Caspi, A. Preventing the Intergenerational Continuity of Antisocial Behavior: Implications of Partner Violence, in D. P. Farrington & J.W. Coid (Eds.), Early Prevention of Adult Antisocial Behavior (Cambridge, UK, Cambridge University Press, 2003), 109-29
9. Consumo de drogas en la población general (Drug consumption in the general population). argentina.gob.ar - https://bit.ly/3a2CD71
10. Kandel E. R. A new intellectual framework for psychiatry. Am J Psychiatry, 1998; 155: 457-69
11. Solomon, C. R. Hacia la felicidad. Casa Bautista de publicaciones, 1978, págs. 26 y 37
12. Collins, G. Search for Reality. Santa Ana, Vision House
13. Padilla, C. R. Holistic Mission, Lausanne Ocasional Paper No. 33: Holistic Mission, 2005, 11-23 https://bit.ly/30RnfLk
14. La salud mental y la iglesia: La gente está buscando misericordia (Mental health and the church: People are seeking mercy). Baptist Press - https://bit.ly/33D09u
15. Stetzer, E. Sermons Stop Stigma, Plenary address via video at the Summit on the Church, Health, and Mental Health (Belhaven University, Jackson, MI, 2016)

Chapter 2

1. Carga global de enfermedad mental en 204 países - IntraMed.net - https://bit.ly/3bwWtHW
2. 2020: Un año desafiante para la salud mental - news.un.org - https://bit.ly/316hYLV
3. La salud mental en cifras - Confederación Salud Mental España - https://bit.ly/3bE80KF
4. La OPS destaca la crisis de salud mental poco reconocida a causa de la COVID-19 en las

5. Américas - Organización Panamericana de la Salud - https://bit.ly/3n190ku
6. 2020: Un año desafiante para la salud mental - news.un.org - https://bit.ly/316hYLV

Chapter 3

1. Brueggemann, W. The Psalms and the Life of Faith: A Suggested Typology of Function, Journal for the Study of the Old Testament, 17 (1980), 3-32

Chapter 5

1. Spurgeon y sus aflicciones. allanroman.blogspot.com https://bit.ly/30N7 8wp
2. La angustia y agonía de Charles Spurgeon - http://www.spurgeon.com.mx/angustias.html
3. Bunyan, John. El Progreso del Peregrino. 2009, Editorial CLIE
4. Freedman, Kaplan y Sadok. Tratado de Psiquiatría, Ed. Salvat, Barcelona, España, pág. 1381
5. Dante Gebel - La iglesia debería ser el lugar más auténtico. diariolibre.com - https://bit.ly/3u6NxQ8

Chapter 6

1. The price of prosociality in pandemic times. socialscience.nature.com - https://go.nature.com/3np1xkn
2. La importancia de las experiencias tempranas de cuidado afectivo y responsable en los menores. redaylic.org - https://bit.ly/3y4zEmu

Appendix II

1. ¿Es la espiritualidad un tema relevante para la salud mental? Universidad Antonio Ruiz de Montoya - https://bit.ly/3Ab2bJP
2. Hummer, R. A., Rogers, R. G., Nam, C. B., Ellison, C. G. Religious involvement and U.S. adult mortality. Demography, 1999; 36: 273-85. Helm, H. M., Hays, J. C., Flint, E. P., Koenig, H. G., Blazer, D. G. Does private religious activity prolong survival? A six-year follow-up study of 3,851 older adults. J Gerontol A Biol Sci Med Sci, 2000; 55: 400-5
3. La espiritualidad en la relación médico-paciente. intramed.net - https://bit.ly/3y3YFh0
4. Comstock, G. W., Partridge, K. B. Church attendance and health. J Chronic Dis, 1972; 25:665-72
5. Damianakis, T., Marziali E. Older adults' response to the loss of a spouse: the function of spirituality in understanding the grieving process. Aging Mental Health, 2012; 16(1):57-66
6. You K. S., Lee H. O., Fitzpatrick J. J., Kim, S., Marui, E., Lee, J. S. et al. Spirituality, depression, living alone, and perceived health among Korean older adults in the community. Arch Psychiatr Nurs, 2009; 23: 309-22
7. O'Laoire S. An experimental study of the effects of distant, intercessory prayer on self-esteem, anxiety, and depression. Altern Ther Health Med, 1997; 3: 38-53
8. Ostrom, R., Watkins, P., Dean, T., Mashburn, D. Comparative efficacy of religious and non-religious individuals. J Consult Clin Psychol, 1992; 60: 94-103

9. Snyder, C. R. The past and possible futures of hope. J Soc Clin Psychol, 2000; 19: 11-28

10. Muris, P, De Jong, P. Monitoring and perception of threat. Pers Indiv Differ, 1993; 15: 467-70

11. Koenig, H. G. Religion, spirituality, and health: a review and update. Adv Mind Body Med., 2015; 29(3):19-22. 5. Moreira-Almeida, A., Koenig, H. G., Lucchetti, G. Clinical implications of spirituality to mental health: review of evidence and practical guidelines. Rev Bras Psiquiatr, 2014; 36:176-82

12. Wachholtz, A. B., Sambamthoori, U. National trends in prayer use as a coping mechanism for depression: changes from 2002 to 2007. J Relig Health, 2013; 52(4):1356-68. do:10.1007/s10943-012-9649-y

13. Las 24 fortalezas personales. Martin Seligman - hittps://bit.ly/3npicPT

SOME QUESTIONS YOU MAY ASK:

WHO IS BEHIND THIS BOOK?

Especialidades 625 is a team of pastors and servants from different countries, different denominations, different church sizes and styles, that love Christ and the new generations.

WHAT IS E625.COM ABOUT?

Our passion is to help families and churches in Latin America to find good materials and resources for discipleship of the new generations and that is why our website serves parents, pastors, teachers, and leaders in general 365 days a year through www.e625.com with free resources.

WHAT IS PREMIUM SERVICE?

In addition to reflections and free short materials, we have a service of lessons, series, research, online books, and audiovisual resources to facilitate your task. Your church can access this service per congregation with a monthly subscription that allows all the leaders of a local church to download materials to share as a team and make the necessary copies that they find relevant for the different activities of the congregation or their families.

CAN I EQUIP MYSELF WITH YOUR HELP?

It would be a privilege to help you and with that objective we have our events and our possibilities of formal education. Visit www.e625.com/Eventos to find out about our seminars and go www.institutoE625.com to learn about the online courses offered by Instituto e6.25

DO YOU WANT CONTINUOUS UPDATES?

Register right now for e625.com updates depending on your field of work: children, preteens, teens, young adults.

LET'S LEARN TOGETHER!